APPETIZERS

Joanna White

BRISTOL PUBLISHING ENTERPRISES
San Leandro, California

A Nitty Gritty® Cookbook

Printed in the United States of America.

ISBN 1-55867-138-2

Cover design: Paredes Design Associates
Cover photography: John A. Benson
Food stylist: Suzanne Carreiro
Illustrator: James Balkovek

CONTENTS

APPETIZER TIPS

An appetizer is not the main course, but a tempting nibble that should excite rather than satiate the appetite. If serving predinner appetizers, the cardinal rule should be: keep it light. If serving a cocktail party or appetizer buffet, a variety of appetizers in a substantial amount is the ruling guide.

Be certain the appetizers complement one another. It is important to balance flavors and textures, hot and cold, raw and cooked, simple and elegant. "Starters" are appetizers that are usually eaten at the table before dinner is served. They often precede a more formal or elegant dinner party.

Overall, one of the most important rules is try to design the menu so the hostess or host can enjoy time with the guests and not be tied to the kitchen. Planning is the key to making a party successful!

APPETIZER GUIDELINES

- Serve a contrast of hot and cold appetizers.
- Offer different textures for food served together, such as crisp vegetables or crackers with a creamy dip.
- Avoid being monotonous with flavor — for example, using onions in every recipe.

- For variety, plan on serving at least one appetizer from each of the following categories: vegetables or fruits, meat or poultry, fish or seafood, and something with cheese.
- A general rule for quantity at cocktail parties is to consider at least 6 appetizers per person per hour. When serving appetizers on trays, always try to supplement with self-help foods like spreads and dips.
- If possible, spread foods around on several tables to encourage socializing.
- When serving a buffet, try to have serving dishes that add height to the presentation. Make sure hot foods are more accessible.
- If appetizers are replacing dinner, count on 10 to 12 "bites" per person, and offer at least 5 to 6 choices.
- Coordinate appetizers with the type of cuisine being served for dinner, such as dim sum before a Chinese meal, or tapas before Spanish cuisine.
- If guests are standing and holding a glass in one hand, consider serving only finger foods so guests won't have to do a balancing act.
- To prevent soggy breads and canapés, spread softened butter or cream cheese over bread before applying the filling. Calculate about $1/4$ pound for every loaf of bread.

THE APPETIZER PANTRY

Prepared foods in jars, bottles, cans and packages provide instant, delicious appetizers for drop-in guests.

anchovies: mash and mix with oil, butter or cream cheese for spreads

artichokes: marinated or plain; serve as is or mix with cream cheese for spreads

barbecue sauce: pour over meats, poultry or cream cheese

breads: crusty breads to dip and spread; dense-textured breads, such as bagels, for sandwiches; flavored breads to dip and spread; pita bread to dip, or to butter, sprinkle with herbs and bake

capers: sprinkle on top of creamy spreads for piquant flavor

caviar: serve to those who appreciate it

cheeses: hard cheeses to shred and sprinkle over fillings on toasted bread; soft cheeses to serve with crackers or to make spreads

chips: variety of potato chips, corn chips and bagel chips

chutneys: add flavor to dips and spreads

corn tortillas: fry or bake into chips or make small filled tortillas from leftovers

crackers: an assortment to serve with dips and cheeses

deviled spreads: ham, chicken or beef; spread on bread rounds or crackers

fish: smoked or not, canned or frozen; serve as is or mix into spreads

green chiles: diced; mix into spreads or sprinkle on cheese dishes

ham: canned; cut into chunks or add to spreads

hard-cooked eggs: chop and add to mayonnaise for spreads

horseradish: add heat to sauces, dips and spreads

marinated vegetables: serve as is

mayonnaise: an essential base for quick-fixes such as spreads

mustards: variety to make sauce, dips and to serve on breads

nuts: variety to serve as is or to caramelize with butter, sugar and/or spices

oils: variety of flavors for frying, creating dips or spreading on bread; mix with flavored vinegars to use as a dip for hearty breads

olives: a variety for serving as is; or chop and add to spreads

onions: cocktail varieties; serve as is

patés: canned or from the deli case to spread on crusty bread, toast or crackers

pepper jellies: serve over cream cheese with crackers

peppers: bottled pickled peppers to serve as is

pesto: mix with cream cheese for spreads

pickles: serve whole or chop and add to spreads and dips

sauces: variety of bottled sauces like teriyaki, garlic sauce, Worcestershire, soy sauce, A-1 and dressings to make dips; Tabasco or other chile sauces add "spike" to all types of recipes

spices: variety for quick recipes

sun-dried tomatoes: serve on top of or mix into bread spreads

vegetables: fresh or bottled, marinated; dip or eat as is

vinegars: variety of flavored vinegars for sauces and dips

water chestnuts: add crunch to dips and spreads

PREPARING AND STORING APPETIZERS

Handy Equipment for Preparation

set of good knives	deep fryer
mixer	graters
food processor	toaster oven
blender	baking sheets

cookie cutters
miniature muffin tins
rolling pin
colander
whisk
melon baller

lemon stripper ("zester")
rubber spatulas
butter curler
brushes
baking pans
piping bags and tips

Helpful Serving Equipment

chafing dish
electric heating tray
slow cooker
fondue pots
napkins
silverware
serving tableware (including
  spreaders and ladles)

wooden skewers
variety of glasses
platters
ovenware dishes
plates
toothpicks

Storage

- Store all appetizers in tightly covered containers to prevent drying.
- Use airtight containers if planning on freezing the appetizers.

- Freeze appetizers in a single layer on a baking sheet. Then stack frozen appetizers with layers of waxed paper between them.
- If using bags for freezing, use only moisture/vapor-proof freezer bags.
- Glass containers with air tight lids are acceptable storage containers for appetizers.
- Party sandwiches can be frozen as long as the filling ingredients can be frozen. Fillings made with butter or cream cheese are ideal for freezing.
- Do not freeze lettuce, fresh vegetables, tomatoes, eggs, mayonnaise, salad dressings, aspics or gelatins.
- Freeze baked pastry shells and toast cups separate from their filling in airtight containers. Before serving, bake in a 350° oven for 10 to 15 minutes before adding filling.
  To make pastry shells: Use dough of choice, and line miniature or regular muffin tins or tart tins. Bake at 350° until brown. Fill immediately or freeze.
  To make toast cups: Trim crust from bread, brush both sides with melted butter and press slices carefully into muffin tins to form cups with 4 uniform points. Toast in a 350° oven until crisp and golden brown. Fill immediately or freeze.

SUPERFAST APPETIZERS

These recipes are designed to be put together in a flash so that you will not be spending all your time in the kitchen and will have time to enjoy your guests. Many of the recipes can be made ahead of time and frozen to have on hand with drop-in guests. Keep a few herbs like parsley, rosemary or thyme in your garden for a quick garnish.

PATÉ MUSHROOMS

Many grocery stores have wonderful delis that offer an assortment of patés. Experiment with paté flavors and pick a favorite for this simple and fast recipe.

60 medium mushrooms
1/4 lb. paté of choice
finely chopped fresh parsley for garnish

Wash and dry mushrooms and cut off stems at base of cap. Mash paté with a fork and fill each cap with a small mound of paté. Broil for 2 to 3 minutes until piping hot. Garnish with a sprinkling of finely chopped parsley.

MARINATED BLUE ONIONS

Makes: 2½ cups

This one is fast to make, but you need to start a couple of days before you plan to serve it. Serve with small rounds of rye or pumpernickel bread. I have found that flat-shaped onions have a tendency to be sweeter than round ones.

½ cup olive oil
2 tbs. lemon juice
1 tsp. salt
1 tsp. sugar
¼ cup crumbled blue cheese
dash pepper
dash paprika
2 cups finely sliced red onions
whole sprigs or chopped fresh parsley for garnish

In a food processor or blender, thoroughly mix all ingredients, except onions. Place onions in an attractive serving dish and cover with processed mixture. Cover and chill for 2 days before serving. Garnish with parsley sprigs or a sprinkling of chopped parsley.

HOLIDAY BRIE

Serve this easy-to-fix appetizer with apple wedges and mild crackers. If desired, garnish with unpeeled apple slices (dipped in lemon juice to prevent browning) and walnut halves.

1 large wheel Brie cheese, 6 lb.
2 medium apples, peeled, cored and chopped
1¼ cups brown sugar
¼-½ cup crumbled blue cheese
1 cup chopped toasted walnuts

Slice Brie in half horizontally. In a bowl, combine apples, brown sugar, blue cheese and walnuts. Spread mixture over Brie half and cover with remaining half. Place on an ovenproof platter and bake at 325° for 20 minutes.

BRIE IN PUFF PASTRY

This recipe makes a beautiful presentation, made easy by using prepackaged puff pastry. The French name for this is Brie en Croute, and it should ideally be served with either fruit or crackers. If you don't buy your Brie in a container, just use the cheese round as a guide.

2 small wheels Brie cheese, 2.2 lb. each
1 pkg. (17¼ oz.) frozen puff pastry, thawed
1 egg yolk
1 tbs. cold water
dash salt

Using the empty Brie container, cut 4 circles out of puff pastry and place a circle on top and bottom of each cheese round. Cut 1-inch strips of remaining pastry and use to encircle cheese sides. Crimp edges together. Beat egg yolk, water and salt together and brush over top and sides of pastry shell. Be creative: cut pastry strips and make a lattice on top of rounds, or cut decorative shapes like leaves and grapes, placing them artfully on top. Brush again with yolk mixture. Chill until ready to bake. Preheat oven to 450° and bake for 10 minutes. Reduce heat to 350° and continue baking for 20 minutes. Crust should be puffed, light and brown.

CHEESY CRAB TOAST

It's very simple, but it tastes elegant. If your budget is a consideration, the "fake" crabmeat can be substituted in a pinch!

4 French rolls
½ cup butter, melted
6-8 tsp. Dijon mustard
12 oz. crabmeat
8 oz. sharp cheddar cheese, shredded
2 tbs. minced fresh parsley
paprika

Cut rolls in half lengthwise and brush with melted butter. Place buttered rolls on a baking sheet and toast under the broiler until golden brown. Remove from oven and spread with mustard. Evenly distribute crabmeat among rolls and sprinkle with cheese. Return baking sheets to oven and broil until cheese melts. Remove from oven and sprinkle with parsley and paprika. Cut rolls into 1-inch diagonal slices and serve immediately.

ANCHOVY BUTTER ROUNDS

Makes: 24

Anchovies create a unique flavor of saltiness, pungency and a bit of the exotic that is appreciated by those with discerning taste buds. Capers are the small buds of plants that grow along the Mediterranean and are packed in a brine. I prefer the smaller bud variety for cooking.

10 anchovies
1/2 cup butter
24 small toasted bread rounds
2-3 tbs. capers

Mash anchovies and mix thoroughly with butter. Chill for at least 1 hour. Spread toasted bread rounds with anchovy butter and sprinkle with capers.

SARDINES AND PEPPER SPREAD

Servings: 6-8

This is a typical Spanish tapa which should be served with a crusty bread or crackers.

2 tins (3.75 oz. each) sardines
½ cup olive oil
2 medium onions, chopped
1 can (4 oz.) roasted red peppers
salt to taste

Rinse sardines in warm water and drain. Pour ¼ cup olive oil in a small baking dish and layer with onions. Top with sardines. Cut red pepper into strips and place over sardines. Sprinkle with remaining olive oil and salt. Bake in a 350° oven for 30 minutes. Serve warm with bread or crackers for dipping.

GRILLED MARINATED PRAWNS

This very simple but elegant appetizer wows your guests. If a barbecue is not available, the prawns can also be quickly sautéed in the same marinade mixture.

1 lb. prawns (18-24 per lb.)
1 cup olive oil
2 cloves garlic, minced
1 tsp. salt
½ tsp. chili powder
1 tbs. chopped fresh parsley

Peel prawns, but leave tails on. Mix remaining ingredients together and pour over prawns. Marinate for 1 hour. Grill prawns on a barbecue grill or under the broiler, basting with marinade.

BACON SCALLOPS WITH BÉARNAISE

These crispy tidbits are dipped in a Béarnaise sauce that can be made in minutes in the food processor or blender.

1 lb. bacon
1 lb. scallops
3 egg yolks
6 oz. butter, melted
salt and pepper to taste

1 tbs. lemon juice
1 tbs. vinegar
1 shallot, minced
1 tsp. mixed tarragon, chervil and
    parsley herbs

Cut bacon slices into thirds and boil for about 5 minutes to remove excess fat and impurities; allow to cool. Wrap each scallop with a piece of bacon and secure with a toothpick. Place on a broiler pan. Broil until nicely browned.

Beat yolks in a food processor until light yellow in color, and add hot melted butter slowly in a stream. Add salt, pepper, lemon juice, vinegar, shallots and herbs. Taste and adjust seasonings and lemon juice.

SMOKED TURKEY ROLL

Makes: 48-60

This is fast and easy to fix. Serve with honey mustard dressing as a dipping sauce.

1 lb. sliced smoked turkey
½ lb. cotto salami, thinly sliced
8 oz. cream cheese, softened
½ red bell pepper, thinly sliced
½ yellow bell pepper, thinly sliced
½ green bell pepper, thinly sliced

Place a slice of smoked turkey on a piece of plastic wrap. Cover with salami, spread with cream cheese and place 1 strip pepper of each color in center. Roll tightly and chill. To serve, cut into ½-inch slices.

TERIYAKI CHICKEN WINGS

This popular recipe will disappear fast when serving a crowd, so be sure to make plenty. Keep it warm in a chafing dish and serve with lots of napkins!

2 lb. chicken wings
1 small onion, chopped
½ cup soy sauce
½ cup brown sugar, firmly packed
1 tsp. minced ginger root
2 cloves garlic, minced
2 tbs. dry sherry
sesame seeds for garnish, optional

Disjoint chicken wings and discard tips. Place wing parts in a baking dish. In a food processor or blender, combine remaining ingredients. Pour over chicken, and if time permits, marinate for at least 1 hour. Bake in a 350° oven for 1 hour. Keep warm in a chafing dish and sprinkle with sesame seeds if desired.

PESTO PARMESAN SWIRLS

Makes: 96

Using bottled pesto and premade puff pastry, these delicious appetizers take just minutes to prepare and are kept frozen until ready to use.

12 oz. cream cheese, softened
1/2 cup grated Parmesan cheese
2 green onions, finely minced
1/4 cup bottled pesto sauce
1 pkg. (17 1/4 oz.) puff pastry sheets

In a food processor or blender, combine cream cheese, Parmesan, minced green onions and pesto together. Lay pastry sheets out and spread with filling. Roll up tightly in jelly-roll fashion. Wrap in plastic and freeze. When ready to bake, thaw rolls for 15 minutes and slice into 1/4-inch rounds. Place on ungreased baking sheets. Bake in a 375° oven for 10 to 15 minutes or until nicely browned.

QUESADILLAS

A quesadilla is a cheesy Mexican delight that is ideally served with a side of guacamole and sour cream for dipping. This is a favorite of every group and should be served with a lot of napkins!

vegetable oil for frying
12 flour tortillas, 8-inch
4 oz. sharp cheddar cheese, grated
4 oz. Monterey Jack cheese, grated
4 green onions, diced
1 can (4 oz.) diced green chiles

Heat a small amount of oil in a medium skillet and place 1 tortilla in pan. Sprinkle with a handful of both types of cheese. Sprinkle with green onions and diced chiles. Cover with another tortilla. When cheese is melted, flip quesadilla over and toast other side. Remove from pan onto a paper towel to absorb oil, cut into 6 wedges and serve immediately. Repeat this technique each time.

SMOKED SALMON ROLLS

Viking bread can be found in most grocery stores, usually in the cracker section. If canned salmon is all that is available, add a few drops of liquid smoke to the recipe. Viking bread is a large, round cracker bread that is usually rye-flavored. If you can't find cracker bread, then thinly slice a round loaf of bread horizontally and remove the crust. It is not necessary to run this under water.

8 oz. cream cheese, softened
1/2 cup butter, softened
4 oz. smoked salmon
2 green onions, chopped
1 pkg. Viking bread

Mix softened cream cheese with butter until smooth. Add smoked salmon and green onions and mix to combine. Run each slice of Viking bread quickly under water until lightly moistened. Spread with salmon mixture and roll up. Wrap tightly in plastic wrap and refrigerate for several hours or overnight. Just before serving, cut into 1-inch pieces.

SPICED MELON BALLS

This makes a cool, refreshing appetizer that takes minutes to prepare and won't fill up your guests before dinner.

1 medium honeydew or Crenshaw melon
1 large cantaloupe
2 tbs. lime juice
2 tbs. honey
½ tsp. ground coriander
½ tsp. nutmeg
fresh mint sprigs or lime slices for garnish

Cut melons in half and remove seeds. Using a melon baller, form fruit into balls and place in bowl with remaining ingredients. Stir to coat and allow mixture to chill for several hours before serving. Garnish with mint sprigs or lime slices and serve with toothpicks.

STUFFED STRAWBERRIES

Refresh your guests with this sweet appetizer, or use this recipe as a light dessert. I like to serve this at tea parties. If desired, surround fruit with attractive greenery such as mint, watercress or well-cleaned greens from the garden.

1 pt. strawberries
8 oz. cream cheese, softened
confectioners' sugar to taste
orange-flavored liqueur to taste: Grand Marnier, Orange Curacao or Triple Sec

Cut stems off berries to create a flat surface that will allow berries to stand upright. Then cut a crisscross slice ¾ of the way down the opposite (pointed) end of each berry and place on an attractive serving dish. In a mixer or food processor, beat cream cheese and flavor with confectioners' sugar and liqueur of choice. Taste and adjust flavor. Place ingredients in a piping bag with a star tip. Pipe cream cheese mixture into the center of each berry.

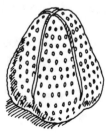

APPETIZERS THAT TRAVEL

Here is a collection of perfect choices for the person who is often called upon to take food to potlucks and other gatherings. Avoid food that needs last minute preparation or baking, so you will not have to inconvenience the busy host.

BRIE IN ASPIC

Brie decorated in this fashion makes a really pretty, very impressive appetizer that will wow your friends. It requires few ingredients. Aspic is a savory jelly made with flavored liquid and unflavored gelatin. Serve with special crackers or rounds of French bread.

2 pkg. (¼ oz. each) unflavored gelatin
½ cup cold water
2 cups Chablis wine
1 large wheel Brie cheese, 6 lb.
pansy flowers (or any edible flowers) for garnish

Soften gelatin in water and heat in a small saucepan until gelatin is dissolved. Remove from heat and add wine, creating aspic. Allow mixture to cool slightly. Brush a layer of aspic on top and along sides of Brie. Artfully arrange flowers on top and gently brush on more aspic. Chill for 5 minutes in the refrigerator and spread on another layer of aspic (only on the top, not on the sides). Repeat this step several times until flowers are completely immersed in aspic. Chill until ready to serve.

FESTIVE BRIE WITH SAVORY STUFFING

Here is another treatment for the always popular Brie, which makes a beautiful, elegant appetizer that can be made ahead of time. Serve with rounds of crispy French bread, or crackers.

1 large wheel Brie cheese, 6 lb.
1 tbs. butter
2 cloves garlic, minced
1 small onion, chopped
8 large mushrooms, finely chopped
½ jar (4 oz.) roasted red peppers, chopped

1 can (4 oz.) sliced black olives
1 tbs. dry sherry
salt and pepper to taste
chopped parsley or chopped red and green bell pepper for garnish, optional

Slice Brie wheel in half horizontally and keep chilled until ready to use. In a skillet, heat butter and sauté garlic and onion until tender. Add mushrooms, peppers and olives and cook for 3 minutes. Add sherry and season to taste with salt and pepper. One hour before serving, spread warm filling over bottom of sliced Brie and cover with remaining half. If desired, sprinkle top of Brie with chopped parsley or peppers.

DATE BREAD WITH PINEAPPLE CREAM CHEESE

Make this sweet appetizer ahead and freeze. Then simply defrost, cut into small rectangular shapes and spread with cream cheese mixture. Garnish the serving platter with colorful flowers.

2 cups boiling water
1 lb. dates, chopped
2 tbs. butter
2 tsp. baking soda
2 cups sugar
3½ cups flour
2 tsp. vanilla
1 cup chopped walnuts
Pineapple Cream Cheese Spread, follows

Line 2 bread pans with brown paper and grease well. In a bowl, mix water, dates and butter together and allow to cool. Add baking soda, sugar, flour, vanilla and nuts, stirring until just mixed. Pour into pans and bake in a 325° oven for 1 hour or until a knife inserted in center comes out clean. Slice bread; cut each slice in half. Spread each slice with *Pineapple Cream Cheese Spread* and arrange on a serving platter.

PINEAPPLE CREAM CHEESE SPREAD

8 oz. cream cheese, softened
1 can (10½ oz.) crushed pineapple, drained
sugar to taste, optional

In a mixing bowl, beat cream cheese and pineapple together. Add sugar if desired.

PUMPKIN TEA SANDWICHES

Makes: 60

This sweet appetizer is ideal during the fall season. Serve with either orange butter or mango spread. This recipe is great for tea parties.

1 cup butter
2 tbs. molasses
3 cups sugar
6 large eggs
1 cup orange juice
1 tbs. grated orange peel
1 can (30 oz.) pumpkin
5 cups flour

1 tsp. baking powder
1 tbs. baking soda
¾ tsp. salt
1½ tsp. cinnamon
1½ tsp. ground cloves
1½ cups raisins or currants
Orange Butter or *Mango Spread*, follow

Line 3 loaf pans with either parchment or brown paper and butter the sides of the pan. With a mixer, cream butter, molasses and sugar until light and fluffy. Beat in eggs until mixture is lemon-colored. Add orange juice, orange peel and pumpkin and mix well. Combine dry ingredients and add to pumpkin mixture, mixing well. Stir in raisins or currants. Spoon mixture into pans and bake at 350° for 1 hour or until a knife inserted in the center comes out clean. Cool in pans for 10 minutes before turning out onto racks. Cut bread into slices and then slices in half. Spread with *Orange Butter* or *Mango Spread*.

ORANGE BUTTER

Makes: ¾ cup

½ cup (1 stick) unsalted butter, softened
¼ cup orange marmalade

With a food processor or electric mixer, mix butter and marmalade until well blended.

Makes: 1½ cups

MANGO SPREAD

8 oz. cream cheese
½ cup mango chutney

Soften cream cheese and stir in chutney.

MARBLEIZED TEA EGGS

This is an elegant alternative to the standard deviled eggs. Using vegetables as natural dyes, the hard-cooked eggs are cracked in the shells and allowed to steep in colored water to create a beautiful marbleized affect. If desired, garnish each egg with a small piece of parsley and a tiny sliver of red pepper.

	18 eggs
	1 tbs. salt
for pink color:	2 cups beet juice
for green color:	3 pkg. (10 oz. each) frozen spinach
	1½ cups water
for yellow color:	4 whole onion skins
	2½ cups water

FILLING

½ cup mayonnaise
3 oz. cream cheese
¼ lb. butter

dash Worcestershire sauce
1 tsp. Dijon mustard
salt and white pepper to taste

In a large saucepan, place eggs, 1 tbs. salt and enough cold water to cover eggs by 1 inch. Bring to a boil. Cover and reduce heat to low. Cook for 20 minutes. Drain at once and chill in ice water for 5 minutes. Crackle egg shells by tapping lightly with back of spoon, rolling gently on surface, or between hands. Leave shells on and dye 6 eggs at a time.

PINK COLOR: Pour beet juice over eggs in a small bowl, deep enough to cover cracked eggs. Allow to steep overnight.

GREEN COLOR: In a saucepan, combine spinach and 1½ cups water and bring to a boil. Reduce heat, cover and simmer for 30 minutes. Strain juice and cool to room temperature. Pour juice over eggs and allow to sit overnight.

YELLOW COLOR: In a saucepan, boil onion skins and 2½ cups water for 20 minutes. Strain juice and cool to room temperature. Pour juice over eggs and allow to sit overnight.

Remove eggs from dye and peel. Split in half in the center *horizontally* (not lengthwise) and cut a little piece off the bottom so the eggs will stand up. Scoop out yolks and combine, using a food processor or mixer, with mayonnaise, cream cheese, butter, Worcestershire, mustard, salt and pepper. Process until smooth; taste and adjust seasonings. Place mixture in a piping bag and pipe into egg halves.

SHRIMP- AND VEGETABLE-FILLED PASTA SHELLS

Makes: 12

Stuffed pasta shells are a quick, unusual and substatial appetizer that can be made ahead of time. Serve on a bed of lettuce. If desired, several of these can be an entrée for a luncheon.

1/2 cup chopped water chestnuts
2 cups chopped celery
2 cups grated carrots
1/4-1/2 cup chopped green onions
2 cups fresh baby shrimp
2 cups shredded sharp cheddar cheese
  (can use low fat variety)

1 cup mayonnaise (prefer low fat or
  nonfat)
1 tbs. lemon juice (or to taste)
1 tsp. sugar
1 lb. jumbo pasta shells, cooked and
  drained

In a bowl, combine water chestnuts, celery, carrots, green onions, shrimp and cheddar cheese. In a separate bowl, blend mayonnaise, lemon juice and sugar. Combine both mixtures and fill shells. Keep refrigerated until ready to serve.

MANGO CHUTNEY MOLD

Cover crackers or plain bagel chips with this creamy, sweet, exotic spread.

12 oz. cream cheese, softened
3 tbs. mayonnaise
3 tbs. chopped peanuts
3-4 tbs. chopped raisins
4 slices bacon, fried crisp and crumbled
1 tbs. chopped green onions
2 tsp. curry powder
1 cup chopped mango chutney
½ cup shredded coconut

Combine cream cheese and mayonnaise in a food processor or with a mixer until smooth. Add remaining ingredients, except chutney and coconut. Lightly oil a 3-cup mold and fill with creamed mixture. Chill for several hours or overnight. To serve, remove from mold, pour chutney on top and sprinkle with coconut.

BLUE CHEESECAKE

A delicious spread always makes a winning appetizer. Serve with rye bread rounds or crackers. Garnish with colorful fresh flowers or carved vegetable flowers, or consider a sprinkling of minced red bell peppers and green onions.

16 oz. cream cheese, softened
8 oz. blue cheese
1/4 tsp. white pepper
2 1/2 cups sour cream
3 eggs
1/2 cup chopped toasted pecans
1/4 cup minced green onions

In a food processor or blender, process cream cheese, blue cheese and white pepper until well blended. Stir in 1 cup of the sour cream, and eggs. Stir in nuts and green onions. Pour mixture into a buttered 9-inch springform pan and bake in a 300° oven for 65 minutes. Remove from oven and let stand for 5 minutes. Spread remaining 1 1/2 cups sour cream over top and return to oven for 10 minutes. Cool completely and refrigerate overnight.

CHEESE TERRINE WITH PESTO
AND SUN-DRIED TOMATOES

Servings: 12

This is a great recipe that can be thrown together in minutes. Both pesto and sun-dried tomatoes are popular flavors, and this recipe has beautiful eye appeal. Serve with crackers or sliced baguettes.

2 lb. cream cheese, softened
8 oz. goat cheese
1 jar (8.5 oz.) sun-dried tomatoes packed in oil
1 bottle (10 oz.) pesto

Combine cream cheese with goat cheese. Line a terrine, mold or loaf pan with a wet cheesecloth. Place 1/5 of the cheese mixture in bottom and spread with 1/2 of the tomatoes. Cover with 1/5 of cheese mixture and spread with 1/2 of the pesto. Repeat layers, ending with cheese mixture. Chill for several hours or overnight. Unmold, remove cheesecloth and serve on a platter.

ROQUEFORT MOUSSE

Another tantalizing spread is delicious with an assortment of crackers and fruit. This goes especially well with pears.

1 cup cream
2 eggs, separated
1 lb. Roquefort cheese,
  room temperature
8 oz. cream cheese

½ cup butter, softened
2 tbs. unflavored gelatin
¼ cup cold water
1 tsp. Dijon mustard

Whip cream and set aside. Beat egg white until stiff and set aside. In a separate bowl, beat egg yolks, add Roquefort and beat until smooth. Add cream cheese and butter and beat until smooth. In a small saucepan, dissolve gelatin in cold water; gently heat and stir until completely dissolved. Add to cream cheese mixture with Dijon mustard. Fold in egg whites. Fold in whipped cream. Pour mixture into a greased 7-cup mold and chill until firm. Unmold to serve.

Note: If you are concerned about the use of raw eggs in your area, increase cream to 1½ cups, and substitute ¼ cup pasteurized eggs, such as Egg Beaters, for egg yolks.

MOLDED HERBED CHEESE

Servings: 10-12

Shape this standard spread into molds to fit the theme of the party. Consider using this mixture to stuff celery sticks or to use as a spread on small, shaped bread slices.

16 oz. cream cheese, softened
6 green onions, chopped
4 cloves garlic, minced
½ cup chopped fresh parsley
½ cup chopped fresh basil
1 tsp. dry mustard
1 tsp. Worcestershire sauce
¼ cup lemon juice
½ cup chopped black olives
salt and pepper to taste

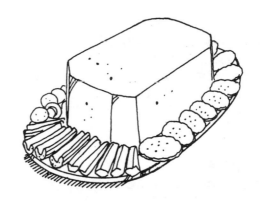

In a food processor or with a mixer, blend ingredients together. Taste and adjust seasonings. Spoon into a 3-cup mold, cover and refrigerate until mixture sets. Unmold onto a platter.

LATTICE CREAM CHEESE MOLD

Servings: 12-15

A favorite spread is a fancy one to take to a party. For a change, try different combinations of cheese and alternative meats in place of the ham. Serve with an assortment of crispy crackers.

FIRST LAYER
8 oz. cream cheese, softened
2 tbs. butter, softened
6 oz. smoked ham, minced
2 dashes Tabasco Sauce

SECOND LAYER
8 oz. cream cheese, softened
2 tbs. butter, softened
1/3 lb. grated sharp cheddar cheese
2 tbs. milk or cream
few drops orange food coloring, optional

THIRD LAYER
8 oz. cream cheese, softened
2 tbs. butter, softened
4 green onions, tops only, finely minced
few drops green food coloring, optional

GARNISH
4 oz. cream cheese, softened
sliced black olives
sliced pimiento

Line a 9-inch springform pan with plastic wrap.

In a food processor or blender, process first layer ingredients until creamy. Spread on the bottom of lined springform. Place pan in freezer.

Process second layer ingredients; add food coloring if desired. When first layer is chilled enough so it won't mix with this layer, spread second layer and return to freezer.

Process third layer ingredients and spread this on top of chilled second layer. Cover with plastic and allow to chill in the refrigerator until well set, at least 1 hour. When ready to serve, remove mixture from pan (green layer should be on top) and place on a serving platter.

Whip 4 oz. cream cheese until soft and place in a piping bag. Pipe a thin lattice of cream cheese across the top of the mold and alternate black olives and pimiento slices at each crisscross section.

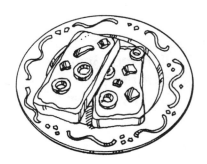

SALMON LOG

This creamy smoked salmon spread can be made far in advance. If you are going to serve this the next day, roll it in the nut mixture about 1 hour before serving. Serve with a variety of crackers or bread rounds.

8 oz. cream cheese, softened
1 can (1 lb.) salmon
2 tsp. minced onion
¼ tsp. liquid smoke
1 tbs. lemon juice
1 tbs. horseradish
¼ tsp. salt
1 cup chopped toasted pecans
2 tbs. chopped fresh parsley

With a mixer, beat cream cheese, salmon, minced onion, liquid smoke, lemon juice, horseradish and salt until well mixed. Shape mixture into a log roll. (If mixture is too soft to form, chill in refrigerator until firm). Mix pecans and parsley together. Roll log in pecan-parsley coating. Cover with plastic wrap and refrigerate until ready to serve.

CHICKEN RELISH SWIRLS

Makes: 24

A good way to use leftover chicken! Make sure the rolls are well chilled before slicing so you can make clean slices. Place these in a single layer on platters and garnish.

8 oz. cooked chicken meat
4 tsp. mango chutney
2 tbs. mayonnaise
1/4 cup chopped green bell pepper
4 green onions, chopped
4 gherkin pickles, chopped

1/4-1/2 tsp. curry
salt and pepper to taste
6 slices bread, crusts removed
1/2 cup butter, softened
1 cup whole stuffed green olives
chopped fresh cilantro for garnish

In a food processor, chop chicken meat into a fine mince. Add chutney, mayonnaise, peppers, green onion, pickles, curry, salt and pepper. Process just enough to combine. Taste and adjust seasonings. Using a rolling pin, flatten bread slices and spread with butter. Spread with chicken mixture and arrange a row of olives along the edge of each slice. Tightly roll up, jelly-roll style, and wrap in plastic wrap. Chill for at least 2 hours. Cut each roll into 4 slices at an angle and garnish with a sprinkling of cilantro.

SMOKED SALMON TREATS

Salmon is a popular flavor and these are relatively quick to fix. Of course, true smoked salmon can be substituted for the salmon and liquid smoke.

8 oz. cream cheese, softened
1 can (7¾ oz.) salmon, skin and bones removed, flaked with fork
4 drops liquid smoke
3 tbs. minced green onion
½ loaf sliced bread
½ cup butter, softened
paprika for garnish

Mix cream cheese, salmon, liquid smoke and green onion together. Remove crusts from bread slices and flatten bread with a rolling pin. Butter ½ of the slices on 1 side and butter remaining slices on both sides. Cut all bread with a small round 2-inch fluted cutter. Spread salmon mixture on bread rounds buttered on 1 side only. Cover each with a round that is buttered on both sides. Sprinkle each buttered top with paprika. Press lightly together and chill until ready to serve.

CUCUMBER MINT COOLERS

Cucumber tea sandwiches make a light and refreshing appetizer. Consider serving this at your next tea party.

1 large cucumber, peeled
1½ tsp. salt
8 tsp. chopped fresh mint
½ tsp. sugar
1 tsp. lemon juice
12 tbs. butter, softened
16 slices bread, crust removed
pepper to taste
mint sprigs for garnish

Slice cucumber very thin and sprinkle with salt. Place in a colander and drain for 30 minutes. Pat dry on towels and set aside. In a food processor or blender, process mint and sugar together until finely minced. Add lemon juice and butter; blend until smooth. Spread mixture on bread slices, place cucumbers on ½ of the bread slices, sprinkle with pepper and cover with buttered bread. Cut each sandwich into 3 long fingers and serve garnished with mint.

BACON-STUFFED CHERRY TOMATOES

This extremely popular appetizer is reminiscent of a BLT. Be aware that they will go fast, so make plenty!

2 lb. bacon
1/3 cup chopped green onions
1/2 cup mayonnaise
24 large cherry tomatoes
lettuce leaves

Finely dice bacon and fry in a skillet until crisp. Drain and cool on paper towels. In a bowl, mix fried bacon pieces, green onions and mayonnaise together. Refrigerate while preparing tomatoes. Cut the bottom (opposite the stem end) from each tomato and scoop out pulp with a melon baller or small spoon. Allow hollowed tomatoes to drain on paper towels. Make sure stems are removed. Fill cavity with bacon mixture and set stem-side down on a serving platter. Surround tomatoes with greens and refrigerate until ready to serve.

CUCUMBERS WITH HERBED CREAM CHEESE

Makes: 36

This is a delicate and refreshing appetizer. The cucumbers can be cut into shapes to follow a theme, such as hearts for Valentine's day.

2 large cucumbers (prefer English variety)
1 clove garlic, minced
1/4 cup chopped parsley
2 green onions, chopped
8 oz. cream cheese
dash Tabasco Sauce
1 tbs. white wine
white pepper to taste
finely minced red bell pepper or fresh parsley sprig for garnish

Peel, slice and, if desired, use a cookie cutter to cut cucumbers into shapes. Using a food processor or blender, blend garlic, parsley and onions until finely minced. Add remaining ingredients and process until well mixed. Taste and adjust seasonings. Transfer ingredients to a piping bag and pipe mixture onto cucumber slices. Garnish and chill until ready to serve.

MARINATED VEGETABLES

Instead of the standard vegetable tray, consider an artful display of marinated vegetables. For additional color, add a variety of black and green olives to the tray. The marinade can be used over again and alternative vegetables may be substituted, such as tomatoes and mushrooms.

1 head broccoli
1 head cauliflower
4-5 carrots
2 cloves garlic, minced
1½ cups vinegar (prefer balsamic)

2½ cups olive oil
1½ tbs. dried dill weed
1½ tbs. sugar
1½ tsp. salt
1½ tsp. pepper

Cut florets from broccoli and cauliflower and cut into bite-sized pieces. Peel broccoli stems and cut into thin slices on the diagonal. Peel carrots and cut into diagonal slices. Place remaining ingredients in a food processor or blender and process until well combined. Taste and adjust seasonings to personal taste. Pour mixture over vegetables, cover and refrigerate overnight.

BARBECUED CHICKEN WINGS

This is a great recipe for traveling, because you simply unplug the Crock-pot and transport it to the party. To help your hostess, consider bringing an extension cord so it can be easily placed. Serve directly from the pot with lots of napkins!

4 lb. chicken wings
2 large onions, chopped
2 cans (6 oz. each) tomato paste
2 large cloves garlic, minced
¼ cup Worcestershire sauce
¼ cup vinegar
½ cup brown sugar
½ cup sweet pickle relish
½ cup red or white wine
2 tsp. salt
2 tsp. dry mustard

Cut off wing tips and discard. Cut wings at the joint and place in a Crock-pot (or other slow cooker). Add remaining ingredients and stir. Set slow cooker on LOW and cook for 5 to 6 hours.

HONEY CHICKEN WINGS

*A nice alternative to teriyaki chicken wings. Be sure to make a large quantity —
this one is very popular.*

3 lb. chicken wings
salt and pepper to taste
1 cup honey
3 tbs. ketchup
½ cup soy sauce
2 tbs. vegetable oil
1 clove garlic, minced
sesame seeds for garnish, optional

Disjoint chicken wings, remove tips and discard. Place chicken pieces in a shallow baking dish and sprinkle with salt and pepper. Mix together remaining ingredients, except sesame seeds, and pour mixture over chicken. Bake in a 350° oven for 50 minutes. Sprinkle with sesame seeds, if desired, and serve warm.

SAUSAGE IN BRIOCHE

Great for picnics or boating. Traditionally, this is served on Bibb lettuce and accompanied by gherkin pickles and Dijon mustard. It goes well with soups and salads.

1 pkg. active dry yeast
3 tbs. warm milk
2 tsp. sugar
½ cup butter, cut into pieces
2 cups flour
1 tsp. salt

2 eggs
1 sausage, 6-7 inches long, about 2 inches in diameter
1 egg yolk mixed with 1 tsp. water and dash salt

Mix yeast, milk and sugar together and let stand for 5 minutes. Add butter, flour, salt and eggs and mix in a food processor for 3 minutes. Transfer mixture to an oiled bowl, and slash top with an X. Cover and let rise until double in bulk. Preheat oven to 400°. Punch dough down and form into a 10-inch rectangle. Trim ends of sausage and encase with dough. Transfer to an oiled baking pan and glaze with egg mixture. Bake for 35 minutes. Cool for 10 minutes before cutting. Cut into 12 slices, about ½-inch each.

TURKEY MEATBALLS

Serve either plain or in any sauce that goes well with beef meatballs. A delicate sour cream sauce is especially nice.

1 lb. ground turkey
2 tbs. mayonnaise
2 tbs. minced onion
salt and pepper to taste
seasoned flour for dipping

In a bowl, mix turkey meat, mayonnaise, onion, salt and pepper together. Roll into small balls, roll in seasoned flour and place on a baking sheet. Bake in a 350° oven for 20 minutes or until no longer pink. Serve with toothpicks.

SWEET AND SOUR MEATBALLS

Instead of barbecued meatballs, consider serving sweet and sour meatballs. You can make this into a meal by serving this recipe over rice.

½ cup breadcrumbs
½ cup milk
1 lb. lean ground beef
¼ cup chopped onion
2 tsp. salt
¼ tsp. pepper
2 eggs, beaten
½ cup flour

2 tbs. butter
1¼ cups cold water
1 tbs. cornstarch
¼ cup sugar
¼ cup vinegar
1 tbs. soy sauce
⅓ cup sliced green and/or red bell peppers

In a bowl, combine breadcrumbs and milk and let stand for 5 minutes. Add beef, onion, 1½ tsp. of the salt, and pepper; combine well. Roll meat mixture into small balls, dip in beaten egg and roll in flour. Heat butter in a skillet and brown meatballs on all sides. In a saucepan, combine water and cornstarch and stir until dissolved. Add sugar, vinegar, soy sauce and remaining ½ tsp. salt. Add meatballs and cook over medium heat until mixture thickens. Add peppers, cover and simmer for 10 minutes. Serve in a chafing dish with toothpicks.

CARAMELIZED NUTS

Makes: 1 pound

The secret to great nuts is soaking them in boiling water and drying them in the oven before you begin the caramelizing process. This method of cleansing the nuts tends to make them more digestible.

1 lb. whole walnuts or pecans
boiling water to cover
2 tbs. vegetable oil
1 tsp. coarse salt
¼-½ cup sugar

Place nuts in a bowl and cover with boiling water. Allow to sit for 30 minutes. Drain and rinse nuts well. Pat dry with a towel and place nuts on a baking sheet. Bake at 300° for 30 minutes and stir. Reduce heat to 250° and check every 10 minutes, stirring each time until nuts no longer have moisture in the center. Remove from oven. Heat oil over medium heat in a large skillet or wok and add nuts. Toss to distribute oil, toss in salt and stir to mix. Add sugar a little at a time and stir until sugar begins to caramelize, stirring constantly. This should take 3 to 4 minutes. Taste, being careful to avoid burning yourself, and determine if you wish to add more salt or sugar. When caramelized, remove from heat and spread out on buttered waxed paper to cool.

APPETIZERS FROM THE OVEN

Baked appetizers that are encased in pastry, such as puff pastry, phyllo dough, yeast dough or homemade pastry, add substance and interest to buffet parties. The advantage is that most of the recipes can be made far in advance and frozen. The disadvantage is that they need to be baked just before serving, so some "kitchen duty" is required. I include at least one hot pastry appetizer whenever possible. Always serve them warm or at least at room temperature, never chilled.

CHEESE STRAWS

Makes: about 24

What makes this special is the ginger, which adds a little heat and spice at the same time. This is a great appetizer at a wine party.

2 cups flour
1 tsp. ground ginger
1 tsp. salt
2/3 cup cold butter, cut into small cubes
2 cups shredded sharp cheddar cheese
1/2 cup toasted sesame seeds
1 tsp. Worcestershire sauce
4-5 tbs. cold water

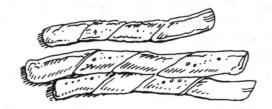

In a food processor or with a mixer, mix together flour, ginger and salt. Add butter and cheese and process to blend. Add remaining ingredients, using enough water to form a stiff dough, and blend until dough forms a ball. Roll dough out on a flour surface and cut into 1/2-inch strips or "straws." Bake in a 400° oven for 10 to 12 minutes or until golden brown.

PHYLLO WITH THREE CHEESES AND WALNUTS

Makes: 72

Wine tasting? Choose this delicate appetizer for a perfect accompaniment.

2 tbs. butter
1 clove garlic, minced
1 onion, finely chopped
1/2 cup crumbled Gorgonzola cheese
2 cups ricotta cheese
1/2 cup shredded Parmesan cheese

1 tbs. basil
1 tsp. ground fennel
1 tsp. nutmeg
1 cup chopped toasted walnuts
1 cup butter, melted
1 pkg. (1 lb.) phyllo sheets

In a skillet, melt 2 tbs. butter and sauté garlic and onion until tender. Remove from heat and mix with cheeses, seasonings and walnuts. Skim top milky layer from melted butter and discard. Brush 1 sheet of phyllo with butter, cut into 3 strips lengthwise, fold each strip in half and brush with butter. Place a spoonful of cheese mixture in top corner and fold in a triangle, like a flag, until a triangular bundle is formed. Brush outside with butter and place on a cookie sheet. Repeat with remaining ingredients. Bake in a 375° oven for 15 to 20 minutes or until golden brown. Serve hot.

RED ONION FOCCACIA

Servings: 12-16

This popular Italian bread has a delicious caramelized onion topping. Make it on a pizza pan and cut it into small squares. This recipe can also be made on the dough cycle of a bread machine.

2 tsp. yeast
1 cup warm water
1 pinch sugar
2½ cups flour
½ tsp. salt
1 tbs. olive oil
1¾ lb. red onions, sliced
⅓ cup olive oil
1 tsp. anchovy paste
1 tbs. white vinegar
olive oil for brushing
salt and pepper to taste

Dissolve yeast in warm water with a pinch of sugar. Add about 1 cup flour to dissolved yeast and beat vigorously for 1 minute. Let rise on a warm oven door until double in bulk, about 30 minutes. Beat mixture down and add salt, remaining flour little by little and 1 tbs. oil. Knead dough well, about 10 minutes. Let rest for 15 minutes.

While dough is resting, cook onions and 1/3 cup olive oil in a skillet over low heat until softened. Dissolve anchovy paste in vinegar and add to onions. Cook over medium heat until onions are soft and liquid has evaporated. Let cool.

Punch down dough and spread in a 12-inch pizza pan. Let rise for 30 minutes in a warm place. Brush dough lightly with olive oil. Sprinkle with salt and pepper. Adjust seasoning of onions and spread gently on dough within 1/2-inch of edge. Bake in a 400° oven for 30 to 35 minutes until lightly browned. Using a pizza cutter or large knife, cut into small squares.

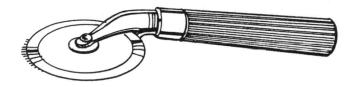

BRIE WAFERS

For a change, you can substitute sharp cheddar cheese for the Brie. This is a great recipe to keep frozen and ready to bake when drop-in guests come a-calling.

½ cup butter
½ lb. Brie cheese, rind removed and cubed
1 cup flour
¼ tsp. seasoning salt
½ tsp. Tabasco Sauce
¼ cup sesame seeds

In a food processor or with a mixer, process butter and Brie until well blended. Add flour, seasoning salt and Tabasco; mix until smooth. Divide dough into 4 parts and shape into logs 1 inch in diameter. Wrap in waxed paper and refrigerate or freeze.

Before serving, slice chilled logs ¼-inch thick. Place slices 1 inch apart on ungreased baking sheets and sprinkle with sesame seeds. Bake in a 400° oven for 8 to 10 minutes or until edges are golden brown. Serve warm.

SPANAKOPITAS

Creamy spinach-filled flaky pastries are a Greek specialty. This recipe can be used as a luncheon entrée by making the pastries considerably larger. These can be frozen and brought out as needed when drop-in guests arrive.

1 pkg. (10 oz.) frozen chopped spinach
2 tbs. butter
1/2 medium onion, chopped
1/2 tsp. nutmeg
salt and pepper to taste

1/2 lb. ricotta cheese
2 eggs, beaten
1/2 lb. butter, melted
1/2 pkg. (1 lb.) phyllo sheets

Defrost spinach and squeeze out excess moisture. Melt butter in a skillet and sauté onion until tender. Add spinach to skillet with nutmeg, salt, pepper, ricotta and eggs. Mix to combine; allow to cool to room temperature. Skim top milky layer from melted butter and discard. Cut phyllo sheets into thirds crosswise. Brush a sheet with butter, place a heaping teaspoon of filling at the corner and fold in half. Brush with butter again and fold in a triangular shape, like a folded flag. Brush outside with butter and place on a baking sheet. Repeat with remaining ingredients. Bake in a 425° oven for about 15 minutes or until golden.

SPINACH AND WALNUT TRIANGLES

Spinach, Swiss cheese and walnuts make a delightful filling that is encased in flaky pastry. There are about 30 sheets of phyllo in a package; refreeze the sheets remaining.

1 pkg. (10 oz.) chopped frozen spinach
1 cup grated Swiss cheese
1 cup chopped toasted walnuts
2 tsp. mustard

1/4 tsp. salt
dash pepper
1/2 cup butter, melted
18 sheets phyllo

Defrost spinach and squeeze out all excess water. Place in a bowl with cheese, walnuts, mustard, salt and pepper and stir to combine. Skim top milky layer from melted butter and discard. Brush 1 sheet of phyllo dough with butter. Divide into thirds, fold each third in half and brush with butter again. Place 1 heaping teaspoon of spinach mixture at end and fold into a triangle. Continue to fold, flag-fashion, back and forth until at end of sheet, brush with butter and place on a baking sheet with sides. Repeat with remaining ingredients. Bake in a 375° oven for 15 to 20 minutes or until golden brown. Serve warm.

OLIVE SWIRLS

A cheese pastry surrounds olives with a slight hint of heat.

½ cup flour
4 oz. cheddar cheese, shredded
3 tbs. butter
dash Tabasco Sauce
½ cup chopped pimiento-stuffed green olives

In a food processor, blend flour, cheese, butter and Tabasco. Form a ball and chill for 30 minutes. Roll dough out to a 6-x-10-inch rectangle between 2 sheets of waxed paper. Sprinkle entire surface with olives and roll up jelly-roll fashion. Wrap rolled dough in waxed paper and allow to chill for 1 hour. Cut roll into ¼-inch slices and place on an ungreased baking sheet. Bake in a 400° oven for about 15 minutes or until golden brown. Serve hot.

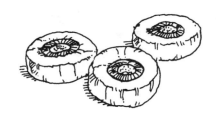

OLIVE PUFFS

Green olives are encased in cheese pastry and served warm. Keep a large quantity of these in the freezer so you won't run out.

2 cups sharp cheddar cheese
½ cup butter
1 cup flour
1 jar (24 oz.) pimiento-stuffed green olives

With a mixer, beat cheese, butter and flour together until well mixed. Roll dough into small balls, press olives in center and cover completely with dough. These can be frozen until ready to bake (thaw before baking). Bake in a 400° oven for 20 minutes or until golden brown.

MUSHROOM STRUDEL TARTS

Makes: 24

Phyllo dough pastry lines little muffin tins and is filled with a mushroom and onion mixture. Try this recipe with different varieties of mushrooms for a delightful change.

4 sheets phyllo
6 tbs. butter, melted, top milky layer
  skimmed off and discarded
1 lb. mushrooms, chopped
½ cup chopped onion
¼ cup chopped fresh parsley
½ cup dry white wine
dash Tabasco Sauce
4 oz. Monterey Jack cheese, shredded

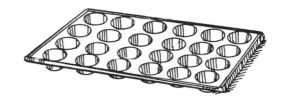

Brush 1 phyllo sheet with butter, cover with another sheet, brush with butter and repeat twice more. Cut phyllo stack into 2-inch squares and place in miniature muffin tins. In a skillet, sauté mushrooms, onion, parsley, wine and Tabasco until liquid is almost evaporated. Cool. Fill muffin cups with mushroom mixture and top with cheese. Bake in a 400° oven for 15 to 18 minutes. Serve warm.

SWEET AND HOT DATE WALNUT WAFERS

Makes: 36

A popular treat is both sweet and hot! This can be frozen and brought out at a moment's notice.

8 oz. sharp cheddar cheese
1½ cups flour
½ cup butter
¼ tsp. cayenne pepper, or to taste
½ tsp. salt
¼ cup white wine

6 oz. pitted dates, chopped
1 cup chopped walnuts
1 beaten egg for glaze
ground walnuts, sesame seeds or
   grated Parmesan cheese for topping,
   optional

In a food processor or by hand using a pastry blender, combine cheese, flour, butter, cayenne and salt. Process until mixture resembles cornmeal. Add white wine and mix until moistened. Cut dates and walnuts into mixture and form into 2 logs. Roll in waxed paper and chill. To bake, cut into thin slices and brush with egg glaze. Either bake as is or sprinkle top with walnuts, sesame seeds or grated Parmesan cheese. Bake in a 375° oven for 10 to 12 minutes or until golden brown.

BLACK-EYED SUSANS

Makes: 36-48

Sweet dates encased in a cheese pastry are a Southern specialty.

1 cup cold butter, cut into small cubes
1 lb. sharp cheddar cheese, shredded
2 cups flour
1 pinch salt
1 pinch cayenne pepper, or more to taste
1 lb. pitted dates
½ cup sugar

In a food processor or by hand using a pastry blender, quickly mix butter, cheese, flour, salt and cayenne together. Taste dough and determine if you wish to add more cayenne. Roll dough into balls and press a date into the center of each, covering it entirely with dough. Roll in sugar and place on a baking sheet. Bake in a 300° oven for 30 minutes. Remove and cool on rack.

SHRIMP PUFFS

Makes: 24

Little cream puffs are filled with a subtle shrimp mixture. Be careful not to fill the puffs until just before serving, so they won't get soggy.

½ cup butter
1 pinch salt
1 cup water
1 cup flour
4 eggs
3 oz. cream cheese
1 jar (4 oz.) olive pimiento cheese
½ cup blue cheese dressing
½ cup mayonnaise
2 tbs. ketchup
¼ tsp. Worcestershire sauce
¼ tsp. horseradish
1 tbs. lemon juice, or to taste
1 clove garlic, minced
1 can (6 oz.) shrimp

In a saucepan, bring butter, salt and water to a boil; remove from heat. Immediately add all flour and stir until dough forms a ball and leaves the sides of the pan. Allow dough to cool slightly. Add eggs, one at a time, and beat very vigorously until a smooth batter is formed. (The beating develops the gluten which makes the puffs rise, so beat very well!) Drop batter by teaspoonfuls onto a greased baking sheet. Bake in a 400° oven for 10 minutes, reduce heat to 350° and bake for another 20 minutes. Remove from oven and cool on wire racks.

Place remaining ingredients in a food processor or blender and process until well mixed. If you prefer, shrimp can be left out of mixture until after blending, and be stirred in by hand to allow them to be seen. To serve, split cooled puffs in half and fill with shrimp mixture.

MINIATURE SHRIMP QUICHES

Makes: 18

Real men, and women, and kids too, love quiche. This is a simple, creamy version with the subtle taste of shrimp.

1 cup plus 2 tbs. flour
½ cup butter
1 tbs. grated Parmesan cheese
1 egg, slightly beaten
dash salt
8 oz. cream cheese, softened

1 tbs. milk
1 tsp. Worcestershire sauce
1 green onion, minced
¼ cup bottled chili sauce
½ lb. shrimp
chopped fresh parsley for garnish

Place flour, butter, Parmesan, egg and salt in a food processor or blender and process until mixed. Wrap dough in plastic and chill. Divide dough into small balls and press each ball into a miniature muffin cup or small tart cup. In a food processor or blender, mix cream cheese, milk, Worcestershire sauce and green onion until smooth. Pour mixture into pastry shells. Top each quiche with a small bit of chili sauce and a few shrimp, and sprinkle with parsley. Bake in a 425° oven for 10 minutes. Remove immediately to a rack to cool.

CRAB IN PHYLLO

Makes: 48

The expense of crab makes this a special treat. These appetizers go especially well with plum sauce, which can be found in the international section of your grocery store. This recipe can be made ahead of time and frozen until ready to bake.

8 oz. cream cheese, softened
4 oz. fresh crabmeat
2 green onions, tops only, finely minced
½ tsp. minced garlic

salt and pepper to taste
few drops Tabasco Sauce
½ pkg. (1 lb.) phyllo sheets
1 cup butter, melted

In a small bowl, gently mix cream cheese, crabmeat, green onions, garlic, salt, pepper and Tabasco to taste. Unroll phyllo. Place a slightly damp cloth over phyllo while working, to keep it from drying out. Skim top milky layer from melted butter and discard. Lightly brush 1 phyllo sheet with butter; cut into 4 strips. Place 1 teaspoon filling in one corner, fold sheet in half and brush with butter. Fold into a triangular shape (flag-fashion), brush triangular bundle with butter and place on an ungreased baking sheet with sides. Repeat with remaining ingredients. Bake in a 350° oven for 15 to 20 minutes or until browned.

CRISPY CRAB ROLLS

This crab-filled flaky pastry has a touch of heat. Make these far ahead of time and bake at the last minute.

4 shallots, minced
¼ cup butter
2 cloves garlic, minced
½ cup chopped fresh parsley
1 tsp. dried dill weed, or more to taste

2 tbs. horseradish
12 oz. crabmeat
1 pkg. (1 lb.) phyllo sheets, or at least
  24 sheets
½ lb. butter, melted

In a skillet, sauté shallots in butter until limp; add garlic, parsley, dill and horseradish. Remove from heat and stir in crabmeat. Taste and adjust seasonings. Skim top milky layer from butter and discard. Butter 1 sheet of phyllo (cover remaining phyllo with a slightly damp towel). Cut buttered phyllo into thirds. Place 1 tbs. of filling at bottom of sheet in the center, roll 1 turn and fold outside edges towards the center, enclosing filling. Brush butter over folded edges and roll up into a long cigar shape. Brush outside with butter and place on a rimmed baking sheet. Repeat for remaining phyllo and filling. Bake in a 350° oven for 15 minutes or until golden. Serve warm.

CRAB TURNOVERS

A creamy crab mixture is flavored with dill and encased in pastry.

1 pkg. (10 oz.) frozen chopped spinach
12 oz. fresh mushrooms, chopped
1/2 cup chopped green onions
1/4 cup butter
1 tsp. salt
1/2 tsp. pepper
1 heaping tbs. flour

12 oz. crabmeat
1/4 cup sour cream
1/4 cup chopped fresh parsley
1 tsp. dried dill weed
1 pkg. (17 1/4 oz.) puff pastry
1 egg, slightly beaten with 1 pinch salt
2-3 tbs. grated Parmesan cheese

Defrost spinach and squeeze out excess moisture. In a skillet, sauté mushroom and onions in butter until soft. Add salt, pepper and flour and cook for about 30 seconds. Gently stir in crabmeat, sour cream, parsley and dill weed. Add spinach to crabmeat mixture. Taste and adjust seasonings. On a floured board, cut pastry dough into 2 1/2- or 3-inch rounds. Brush pastry with beaten egg and place 1 tbs. filling in center. Sprinkle with Parmesan, fold in half and crimp edges with a fork. Brush top of each turnover with more beaten egg and prick with a fork. Place on a baking sheet and bake in a 425° oven for 30 minutes or until golden brown.

SAUSAGE ROLL

Makes: 120

This recipe is perfect for a crowd. It is important to choose a very tasty Italian sausage, since it is the main ingredient. If you prefer a little heat, then choose a hot sausage variety.

1 lb. ground Italian sausage
1/2 medium onion, chopped
1/2 tsp. salt
1/4 tsp. pepper
1 1/2 tbs. basil
1 pkg. (17 1/4 oz.) frozen puff pastry, thawed
1/4 lb. provolone cheese, shredded

In a skillet, cook sausage with onion, salt, pepper and basil until pink color is just gone. Roll each puff pastry sheet into a 15-inch square and cut in half lengthwise. Divide filling into 4 parts and spread over each pastry sheet. Sprinkle with cheese and roll tightly. Chill rolls for at least 30 minutes. Cut into 1/2-inch rounds. Place on an ungreased baking sheet. Bake in a 375° oven until golden brown, about 15 to 20 minutes. Serve warm.

PUFF PASTRY PORK SWIRLS

Make this very tasty, easy-to-make recipe far in advance and freeze it. This is a great recipe that can be made in bulk for large parties.

1 pkg. (1 lb.) frozen puff pastry
1 lb. ground pork
2 tsp. ground cumin
1 tsp. dried thyme
1 tbs. minced garlic
1/4 cup finely chopped green onions
1/4 cup finely chopped red bell peppers or pimiento
salt and pepper to taste
1 egg, slightly beaten with 1 pinch salt

Allow pastry to defrost on counter for several minutes until just pliable. Roll pasty to 1/8-inch thick. Cut into strips about 3 inches wide. Place on cookie sheets sprayed with cold water and refrigerate while making filling. In a bowl, mix pork with remaining ingredients, except egg. Divide filling among pastry strips, spreading filling over top of pastry. Brush edges with water and roll up. Refrigerate or freeze. Just before serving, cut rolls into 1/2-inch sections. Paint with egg wash and bake in a 375° oven until golden, about 15 minutes. Serve warm.

HONEY LAMB PUFFS

A Middle Eastern delight has a very satisfying, piquant quality.

¼ cup raisins
enough hot water to cover raisins
¼ cup olive oil
1¾ cups finely chopped onions
1 tbs. minced garlic
1 lb. ground lamb
2 tsp. salt
1½ tsp. pepper

1 tsp. cinnamon
⅛ tsp. cayenne pepper
¼ cup tomato paste
1 cup chopped fresh tomatoes
⅓ cup honey
1 pkg. (17¼ oz.) frozen puff pastry,
  thawed

Cover raisins with hot water to plump. Heat olive oil in a skillet, add onions and garlic and sauté until tender. Add lamb, salt, pepper, cinnamon and cayenne; cook until meat is no longer pink. Add tomato paste, tomatoes, raisins (which have been drained) and honey. Allow mixture to simmer for several minutes, taste and adjust seasonings. Allow filling to cool. Cut each puff pastry sheet into 16 squares and line miniature muffin tins with pastry squares. Place about 2 tsp. filling in each shell. Bake in a 375° oven for about 20 minutes or until golden. Serve warm or at room temperature.

INTERNATIONAL APPETIZERS

Because of the rich, diverse heritage of the American "melting pot" population, we greatly appreciate the cuisines of other countries. Use appetizers that set the tone. Serve like with like, both in terms of the cuisine (such as Spanish tapas with a Spanish meal) and in terms of style (elegant appetizers with an elegant meal).

PORK SATAY WITH PLUM SAUCE

Servings: 12

Satays have become very popular. Plum sauce is a perfect accompaniment to pork, but can also work as well with beef or chicken. If time is limited, plum sauce is now available in most grocery stores in the international section. Presoak bamboo skewers so they won't burn.

6 cloves garlic, minced
1 tbs. ground coriander
1 tbs. turmeric
1 tbs. brown sugar
1 tbs. ground cumin
1 tsp. white pepper
1 tsp. salt
½ cup coconut milk
2 lb. pork tenderloin, thinly sliced
fresh pineapple, cut into ½-inch wedges
Plum Sauce, follows

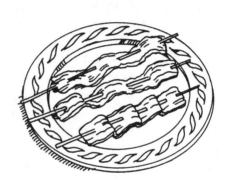

Combine garlic, coriander, turmeric, brown sugar, cumin, white pepper, salt and coconut milk in bowl. Marinate pork slices in this mixture for several hours or, ideally, overnight. Thread pork onto presoaked wooden skewers and top each with a pineapple slice. Grill or broil until done, about 3 to 6 minutes. Serve with *Plum Sauce*.

PLUM SAUCE

This is a fast recipe for plum sauce. The secret ingredient is Chinese 5-spice powder, which can be obtained in Oriental groceries and now in many grocery stores.

2 cups plum preserves
¼ cup rice vinegar
2 tsp. Chinese 5-spice powder
1 tbs. instant chicken bouillon granules
1 tbs. soy sauce

Combine all ingredients and microwave on HIGH for 3 minutes. Stir well and cook for an additional minute. Store in refrigerator until ready to use.

CHICKEN EMPANADAS

Makes: 24

A delicious Mexican treat is now made easier with the advantage of buying frozen puff pastry. If you prefer a spicier mixture, increase the pepper flakes.

⅓ cup raisins
1 cup hot water
3 tbs. vegetable oil
⅔ cup minced onion
1 lb. diced uncooked chicken
¾ tsp. red pepper flakes
1½ tsp. salt
¼ tsp. cinnamon
1 tsp. ground cumin
2 tbs. butter
2 tbs. flour
1 cup chicken stock
3 tbs. chopped green olives
1 pkg. (17¼ oz.) puff pastry
1 egg, beaten
3 tbs. toasted slivered almonds

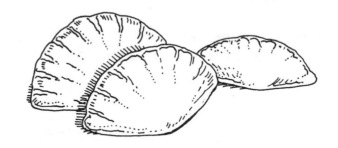

Soak raisins in hot water until plump. Drain. In a skillet, heat oil and sauté onion until soft. Add chicken, pepper flakes, salt, cinnamon and cumin. Cook for 5 minutes. In a small saucepan, heat butter until melted, stir in flour until smooth, add chicken stock and cook until thick. Stir in chicken mixture with raisins and green olives and allow mixture to cool to room temperature.

Roll puff pastry to ⅛-inch thick and cut into 3-inch rounds. Divide filling among rounds and brush edges with water. Fold rounds in half, shape into crescents and crimp edges with a fork. Lay crescents on a lightly buttered baking sheet, brush with lightly beaten egg and sprinkle with toasted almonds. Bake in a 375° oven for 20 to 30 minutes or until golden.

POT STICKERS

Makes: 30

An Oriental dim sum pastry is gobbled up by the guests! An important ingredient is sesame oil, which gives it the special, unique flavor.

2 tsp. minced ginger root
2 green onions, finely minced
6 tbs. cream sherry
1 lb. ground pork
2 tbs. soy sauce
1 tsp. salt
¼ tsp. pepper
1 tsp. sugar
3 tbs. sesame oil
½ cup chopped water chestnuts
1 tbs. chopped fresh cilantro
1 pkg. round won ton wrappers
3 tbs. vegetable oil
1 tbs. white vinegar
1 cup water

Mix together ginger root, green onions and 4 tbs. of the cream sherry. Let stand for 10 minutes; drain. Add pork, soy sauce, salt, pepper, sugar, 1 tbs. sesame oil, water chestnuts and cilantro, mixing to combine. Place 2 tsp. of this filling in center of each wrapper. Dampen edges with water and fold in half. Pleat or crimp edges together. Heat 3 tbs. oil in a large skillet, arrange dumplings in circles in skillet, cover and fry over medium heat for 3 minutes. Combine remaining cream sherry and sesame oil with vinegar and water. Add to fried dumplings and cook uncovered until water is absorbed. An average skillet can hold about 15 dumplings, so split vinegar mixture between 2 pans if desired.

SWEET AND SOUR PUPUS

This Hawaiian favorite can be made ahead of time and baked just before the guests arrive. Scallops or cooked chicken livers can be substituted for the water chestnuts.

1 lb. bacon, cut into thirds
2 cans (8 oz.) whole water chestnuts
¾ cup pineapple juice
1½ tbs. cornstarch
½ cup brown sugar, firmly packed

½ cup cider vinegar
1 tsp. salt
4 tsp. ketchup
1 cup crushed pineapple, drained
few drops red food coloring, optional

Blanch bacon in boiling water for several minutes to remove excess fat. Remove bacon from water and allow to cool. Wrap bacon around water chestnuts and fasten with a toothpick. Place in an ovenproof dish. In a saucepan, mix pineapple juice with cornstarch and bring to a boil. Add remaining ingredients, adding food coloring for eye appeal, if desired. Allow mixture to thicken slightly. Pour sauce over bacon-wrapped water chestnuts. Bake in a 350° oven for 30 minutes and serve immediately.

HAWAIIAN MUSHROOMS

This is an elegant "sit-down" appetizer (or starter) that is rich and creamy. Serve with crusty rolls. To set the ambiance, use a centerpiece with exotic Hawaiian flowers to dress the table.

1/4 cup butter
3 large sweet onions, thinly sliced
16 very large mushrooms
4 oz. fresh crabmeat
1 green onion, finely chopped
3 oz. cream cheese
salt and pepper to taste
1/4 lb. Monterey Jack cheese, shredded

Melt butter in a skillet and sauté onions until golden brown. Place mixture in bottom of a casserole dish or in 8 individual ramekins. Cut stems from mushrooms just at cap level. Place mushrooms in casserole or ramekins. Mix together crabmeat, green onion, cream cheese, salt and pepper. Fill center of mushrooms with crabmeat mixture. Bake in a 350° oven for 5 to 8 minutes or until mushrooms are softened. Sprinkle with cheese and continue to bake until cheese melts. Serve immediately.

TACO SNACKS

Makes: 72

This simple appetizer can be made ahead of time and kept frozen until ready to bake. This one is especially appreciated by children.

1 lb. ground beef
1/3 cup chopped onion
1 pkg. (1.25 oz.) taco seasoning mix
1 tsp. Tabasco Sauce
1/4 tsp. cayenne pepper
1 cup shredded cheddar cheese
3 pkg. refrigerated crescent rolls

In a skillet, brown beef and onion together until no longer pink; drain off excess fat. Add taco mix, Tabasco and cayenne pepper. Taste and add more seasonings if desired. Add cheese and stir until melted. Allow mixture to cool before filling dough.

Roll each package of dough into a large square and cut into 24 squares. Place 2 tsp. filling in center of each square. Pinch 4 corners together and 4 seams. Bake in a 375° oven for 20 minutes or until golden brown.

ITALIAN-STYLE MEATBALLS

Makes: 24

The Italian name for meatballs is "polpette." This particular recipe is from Northern Italy and can be served with your favorite Italian meat sauce, sour cream sauce or, if desired, barbecue sauce.

1 slice bread soaked in milk
1 lb. ground chuck
¼ cup grated Parmesan cheese
¼ cup minced onion
2 cloves garlic, minced
1 tbs. grated fresh lemon peel (zest)
¼ cup minced fresh parsley
1 egg, beaten
salt and pepper to taste
sauce of choice: tomato sauce, meat sauce, sour cream sauce, barbecue sauce

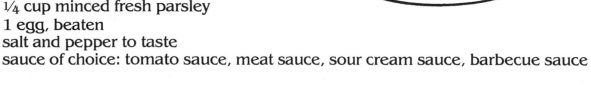

Squeeze milk from bread and place in a bowl. Add remaining ingredients and mix together thoroughly. Fry a small amount of mixture and taste; adjust seasoning to personal preference. Roll mixture into balls and place under the broiler or fry in a skillet until brown on all sides. Put meatballs in sauce of choice and simmer for 1 hour.

CROSTINI OLIVE SPREAD

This recipe makes an Italian favorite that is piquant and can be quite filling. Serve it on toasted bread rounds and, if desired, sprinkle with a little shredded Parmesan and broil until cheese is melted.

1 can (6 oz.) pitted black olives
1 tbs. minced onion
2 tbs. minced fresh parsley
2 tbs. lemon juice
2 cloves garlic, minced
4 anchovies
¼ cup olive oil
salt and pepper to taste
shredded Parmesan cheese, optional

Place all ingredients in a blender or food processor, except Parmesan, and chop until barely mixed. Adjust seasoning to personal taste. Chill until ready to serve. If desired, spread filling on toasted bread rounds and sprinkle with Parmesan. Place under the broiler until cheese melts.

CAPONATA (EGGPLANT ANTIPASTI)

A healthy Italian and French appetizer is made from fresh vegetables. Serve with rounds of crusty French bread. This can be served either hot or cold. It also can be used as a vegetable side dish.

1 medium eggplant
salt
1/4 cup olive oil
1 medium zucchini
1 large onion, diced
3 cloves garlic, minced
1/2 cup diced celery
1 large carrot, diced
1 green bell pepper, seeded and diced
1 1/2 cups chopped tomatoes, drained

3 tbs. tomato paste
1/4 cup chopped fresh parsley
1 1/2 tsp. dried basil
1/4 cup red wine vinegar
2 tsp. sugar
1/4 cup chopped stuffed green olives
1/4 cup chopped pitted black olives
2 tbs. coarsely chopped capers
salt and pepper to taste

Remove peel from eggplant and dice. Sprinkle with salt and place in a colander to drain for 30 minutes. Heat oil in large pan, add eggplant and zucchini and cook until lightly browned. Stir in onion, garlic, celery and carrot and cook for another 10 minutes. Add remaining ingredients and simmer gently for 1 hour. Correct seasonings if necessary.

MIDDLE EASTERN DELIGHTS

A vegetarian appetizer is surrounded by flaky pastry. This can be made ahead of time and kept frozen until ready to bake.

½ medium onion, diced
⅓ lb. mushrooms, diced
2 tbs. butter
1 tbs. chopped fresh cilantro
1 tbs. chopped fresh parsley

1 tsp. ground cumin
½ tsp. salt
¼ tsp. pepper
1 cup butter, melted
16 sheets phyllo (about ½ pkg.)

In a skillet, sauté onions and mushroom in butter until limp. Remove from heat and let cool. Add cilantro, parsley, cumin, salt and pepper. Taste and adjust seasonings. Skim top milky layer from butter and discard. Brush 1 sheet of phyllo with butter, place a second sheet on top and brush again with butter. Cut dough into 3 pieces and place about 1 tbs. filling in the center on one end. Fold sides over filling and roll cigar fashion. Brush outside with butter and place on a rimmed baking sheet. Repeat for remaining ingredients. Bake in a 375° oven for 20 minutes or until golden brown. Serve warm.

FRENCH CAVIAR POTATOES

A simple and elegant presentation — arrange the potatoes in a bed of shredded lettuce or parsley and, if desired, use two colors of caviar for eye appeal and variety.

60 tiny new potatoes, cooked until tender
oil for deep frying
8 oz. sour cream
1 jar (2 oz.) caviar, rinsed and drained

Slice off a small piece of each potato so that it will sit flat. Scoop center out using a melon baller. Heat oil in a deep fryer to 375°, drop in prepared potatoes and fry until crispy. Drain on paper towels and keep warm on a cookie sheet in a low oven until ready to serve. Just before serving, fill with sour cream and top with a small amount of caviar.

TERIYAKI CHICKEN SKEWERS

Makes: about 30

Make this great recipe ahead of time, and it takes just minutes to broil before the guests arrive. Brandied Mayonnaise makes a delightful change from the ordinary.

3½ lb. boneless chicken breast
¼ cup soy sauce
1 tbs. molasses
1½ cups dry white wine
1 cup water

2 tsp. salt
2 tsp. pepper
2 tsp. minced garlic
1 medium onion, minced
Brandied Mayonnaise, follows

Cut chicken breast meat into thin strips and thread onto wooden skewers. Place in a shallow pan. In a bowl, combine remaining ingredients and pour over chicken strips. Marinate overnight. Broil chicken pieces for about 3 minutes on each side and serve on a bed of shredded lettuce either alone or with a bowl of *Brandied Mayonnaise*.

BRANDIED MAYONNAISE

Makes: 1 cup

¾ cup mayonnaise
1 tbs. brandy
3 tbs. ketchup
1 tbs. Worcestershire sauce

1 tbs. honey
1 tbs. lemon juice
salt and pepper to taste

Combine all ingredients. Taste and adjust seasonings. Chill before serving.

GREEK CHEESE PUFFS

A delightfully unique cheese combination has a slight sweetness. These can be made ahead of time and frozen until ready to bake. If you cannot find these delicious cheeses at your grocery, try a Greek deli, or use all feta or add some cream cheese and Parmesan.

½ lb. feta cheese
½ lb. Mizithra cheese
½ lb. kasseri cheese
½ cup honey
¼ tsp. cinnamon
2 eggs
about 1 pkg. (1 lb.) phyllo dough, or 24 sheets
1½ cups butter, melted

In a bowl, mix cheeses, honey, cinnamon and eggs together. Brush 1 sheet of phyllo with melted butter and cut into 3 parts. Fold each part in half and brush with more butter. Place 1 tsp. filling at one end and fold into triangles, flag-fashion, back and forth to end of strip. Butter outside of dough bundle and place on a rimmed baking sheet. Bake in a 375° oven for 12 to 15 minutes or until golden brown and puffed.

HOISIN SPARERIBS

These are a delightful change from the common teriyaki chicken wings. You may have to find an Oriental grocery for a few of the ingredients in this recipe.

3 lb. pork spareribs
2 cloves garlic, minced
½ tsp. minced ginger root
2 tbs. hoisin sauce
1 tbs. ground bean sauce
2 tbs. sugar
¼ cup soy sauce
¼ cup dry sherry
¼ tsp. Chinese 5-spice powder
½ cup water

Have the butcher cut the ribs crosswise into 1½-inch strips. Place ribs in a foil-lined shallow baking pan. Mix remaining ingredients together, except water, and pour over ribs. Marinate for 1 hour. Add water to pan and cover with foil. Bake in a 300° oven for 2½ to 3 hours. Serve warm.

ORIENTAL SHRIMP TOAST

Makes: 32

This popular appetizer should be fried just before the guests arrive. Another possibility is to have a fondue pot with hot oil and allow the guests to cook their own.

8 slices white bread, square loaf
1 lb. cooked shrimp, shelled and deveined
1½ cups finely minced onions
½ tsp. minced ginger root
1 tsp. salt
2 tsp. cornstarch
1 egg
sesame seeds for dipping, optional
oil for deep frying

Trim crusts from bread and cut into 4 triangles. Allow bread to dry for 1 to 2 hours. Mash or finely chop shrimp. In a bowl, mix shrimp, onions, ginger, salt, cornstarch and egg into a smooth paste. Spread shrimp paste on toast. If desired, dip triangle in sesame seeds. Heat oil to 350° and fry bread until both sides are golden brown. Drain on paper towels and keep warm in oven until ready to serve.

PATÉ WITH ASPARAGUS MAYONNAISE

Servings: 12

A pork-and-beef-based paté has asparagus dotted throughout. Serve this with crusty French bread and a side dish of Asparagus Mayonnaise.

1 lb. ground pork
1 lb. lean ground chuck
1 cup fresh breadcrumbs
1 pkg. (10 oz.) frozen chopped spinach,
  thawed and squeezed dry
1 tsp. sage
1 tsp. thyme
2 tsp. salt

1 tsp. pepper
1 tsp. ground rosemary
2 cloves garlic, minced
1 tbs. chopped fresh parsley
few spears fresh asparagus, barely cooked
lettuce leaves
Asparagus Mayonnaise, follows
chopped parsley for garnish

With the exception of asparagus, lettuce leaves, mayonnaise and parsley, mix all ingredients together thoroughly. Press part of the meat mixture into a loaf pan and place whole spears of asparagus throughout meat mixture for color. Bake on a 350° oven for 45 to 55 minutes. Test with a meat thermometer: it should read 170° if done. Remove from oven, place a weight on meat mixture and chill overnight. To serve, remove weight, unmold paté, slice off several pieces and place on a serving dish lined with lettuce. Spoon a line of *Asparagus Mayonnaise* down the center and sprinkle with chopped parsley. Serve with remaining mayonnaise in a dish.

ASPARAGUS MAYONNAISE

Makes: 2 cups

This mayonnaise can also be used as a dressing for pasta salads, sandwich spreads or mixed with filling for deviled eggs.

¼ lb. asparagus, cooked
1½ cups mayonnaise
¼ tsp. dry mustard

Place asparagus in a blender or food processor, puree until smooth and set aside. In a blender or food processor, place mayonnaise and mustard. Add asparagus puree and process briefly to blend. Taste and adjust seasonings. Chill until ready to use.

SESAME WALNUT CHICKEN STRIPS

Makes: 40

The traditional way of seasoning the chicken is with ground roasted Szechwan peppercorns, which creates a unique, fragrant taste sensation. If desired, serve with a homemade sweet and sour sauce.

4 whole chicken breasts, boned and skinned
2 cups walnuts
2 cups sesame seeds
oil for deep frying
salt and pepper (ideally roasted Szechwan pepper) to taste
Sweet and Sour Sauce, follows, optional

Split chicken breasts in half and cut each half into 5 long slivers. In a food processor or blender, process walnuts and sesame seeds together until finely ground. Heat oil to 350°. Dip chicken pieces into nut mixture and drop into hot oil. Fry for several minutes, turning once until golden brown. Remove from oil, drain on paper towels and sprinkle with salt and pepper. Cut strips into small diagonal pieces. Serve with *Sweet and Sour Sauce* if desired.

SWEET AND SOUR SAUCE

¾ cup pineapple juice
1½ tbs. cornstarch
½ cup brown sugar, firmly packed
1 tsp. salt
½ cup cider vinegar
¼ cup ketchup
1 cup crushed pineapple, drained
few drops red food coloring, optional

In a saucepan, mix pineapple juice with cornstarch. Add remaining ingredients and bring to a boil over medium-high heat, stirring constantly until mixture thickens. Remove from heat and serve.

PIROSHKI

This Russian traditional favorite can be made ahead and frozen. This is a hearty appetizer that is really appreciated by male guests. Consider using this recipe as a great picnic entrée in place of sandwiches by cutting larger rounds out of the pastry.

1 cup butter, softened
1 cup sour cream
2½ cups flour
1 tsp. salt
3 tbs. butter
2 onions, finely chopped
1 lb. lean ground beef
2 tbs. sour cream

¼ cup cooked rice
1 tbs. dried dill weed
¼ cup chopped fresh parsley
1 tsp. salt
½ tsp. pepper
2 hard-cooked eggs, chopped
1 egg beaten with 1 tsp. water

Blend 1 cup butter with sour cream; stir in flour and salt. Form dough into a ball, wrap and chill for 2 hours. In a skillet, heat 3 tbs. butter and sauté onion until golden brown. Add beef and cook until meat is no longer pink. Remove from heat and drain off excess fat. Add all other ingredients, except beaten egg, stir to combine and cool to room temperature. Roll dough to ⅛-inch thickness. Cut into 3-inch rounds and place a small amount of filling in center of each, fold over and seal edges. Brush filled pastry with beaten egg and place on a greased baking sheet. Bake in a 400° oven for 15 to 20 minutes or until golden brown. Best served warm.

FRIED CHEESE SQUARES

A favorite Greek appetizer is typically served with retsina wine and crusty bread.

1½ lb. Kefalotyri cheese (or kasseri, Asiago or Romano)
¼ cup olive oil
¼ cup butter
3 large eggs, beaten with a little water
1 cup flour for dredging
2 tbs. brandy
2 tbs. lemon juice
oregano (preferably Greek)
chopped fresh parsley
lemon wedges for garnish

Put an ovenproof dish in a [400°] oven to heat thoroughly while preparing cheese. Cut cheese into 12 squares or triangles ¼-inch thick. In a skillet, heat oil and butter. Dip cheese in beaten eggs, roll in flour and place in heated oil. Fry over medium heat until golden brown on both sides. Remove to heated ovenproof dish. Heat brandy in a small saucepan and pour over cheese; immediately ignite. When flames have died down, sprinkle with lemon juice, oregano and parsley and serve immediately, garnished with lemon wedges.

FRENCH QUICHE TARTLETS

Makes: 1½ quarts

How could men <u>ever</u> say they don't eat quiche! Especially this recipe! These are best served slightly warm. This recipe can be baked and frozen, and reheated at the last moment.

2 cups flour
1 pinch salt
6 oz. butter
⅓ cup cold water
8 slices bacon
1 medium onion, diced
¼ cup chopped green chiles, optional
¼ cup shredded Swiss cheese
¼ cup shredded cheddar cheese
4 large eggs, beaten
1 cup milk
1 cup cream
¼ tsp. nutmeg
½ tsp. salt
¼ tsp. pepper

Place flour, salt, and butter in a food processor and process until crumbly. Add water and process until dough just holds together. Wrap in plastic and refrigerate for 30 minutes.

Roll pastry dough to $\frac{1}{8}$-inch thick, cut with a $1\frac{1}{2}$-inch round cookie cutter with fluted edges and line miniature muffin tins with pastry dough. Chill while making filling.

Cut bacon into a fine dice, fry in a skillet until crisp and drain on paper towels. Fry onion in bacon fat until wilted. Distribute bacon, onion, chiles and cheeses among pastry shells. In a bowl, combine eggs, milk, cream, nutmeg, salt and pepper. Pour mixture into pastry shells. Bake in a 450° oven for 10 minutes. Reduce heat to 350° and bake 8 minutes longer.

MARINATED OLIVES

This recipe gives American olives a Greek flavor. This makes a great gift to give friends for the holidays.

1 lb. large black olives
3 stalks celery, finely chopped
3-4 cloves garlic, minced
juice of 2 lemons
1 whole lemon, cut into small pieces
1 cup olive oil
1½ cups balsamic vinegar or red wine vinegar
2 tbs. dried oregano

Drain olives and, if they are not pitted, slit one side with a knife to allow marinade to penetrate olive. Mix remaining ingredients together and stir into olives. Pack entire mixture into jars, making sure liquid completely covers olives. Add a little water if necessary. Cover and allow to marinate for 2 to 3 weeks, shaking jars every few days.

TARAMASALATA

A Greek fish roe dip is just now becoming popular. The tarama can usually be found in a Greek deli. Serve with hot pita bread or toasted bread.

⅓ jar (8 oz.) tarama (fish roe)
1 small onion, finely grated
1½ cups olive oil, or more if desired
5 slices white bread, crusts removed
⅓ cup fresh lemon juice, or to taste
fresh oregano for garnish

Place tarama and onion in a bowl and mash together. Add a small amount of olive oil very slowly, creating a paste. Moisten bread with a little water, squeeze out excess and beat into tarama mixture alternately with remaining olive oil and lemon juice until a cream-colored mixture is obtained. The quantity of olive oil is determined by how thin or thick you prefer the dip to be. Taste and adjust seasonings. Serve garnished with fresh oregano.

GRECIAN ARTICHOKES

Servings: 6

Serve with crackers or bread rounds. This dish can also be used as a vegetable side dish; simply leave the artichoke hearts whole after thawing.

¾ cup white wine
¾ cup water
¼ cup lemon juice
¼ cup olive oil
2 bay leaves
¼ tsp. dried thyme
salt and pepper to taste
2 pkg. (10 oz. each) frozen artichoke hearts, thawed
1½ tbs. anchovy paste

In a bowl, mix wine, water, lemon juice, olive oil, bay leaves, thyme, salt and pepper together. Cut artichokes into quarters and cook in wine marinade until tender. Remove from heat, cover and marinate overnight in the refrigerator. Remove artichokes from marinade and set aside. In a saucepan, stir anchovy paste into marinade and reduce over medium heat until mixture thickens. Spoon mixture over artichokes and serve either at room temperature or chilled.

LOW FAT APPETIZERS

It is wise to serve at least one healthy, low-fat dish at a party because someone is always dieting, and so many people are conscious of their health. The grocery stores now have so many new ingredients available, such as low fat and fat-free mayonnaise, cream cheese, yogurt, etc., that it is easy to transform your old fat-laden recipes into a healthy alternative. Keep in mind that many of these new products do not work well in recipes that require long cooking or baking times.

HERBED MUSHROOMS

Servings: 20

If desired, once you have added all the ingredients to the pan, remove from heat and refrigerate for up to 2 days before continuing the cooking process.

3 lb. mushrooms
½ cup chicken broth
1 large onion, finely chopped
2 tsp. basil
2 tsp. oregano
½ tsp. thyme

2 cloves garlic, minced
dash Tabasco Sauce
½ cup dry sherry
¼ cup lemon juice
salt to taste

Cut stems from mushrooms at base of cap; use only caps for this recipe. In a skillet, heat chicken broth, add onion and mushrooms and cook until limp. Add remaining ingredients and cook uncovered until liquid is reduced to ½ cup, stirring occasionally. Serve hot in a chafing dish; provide toothpicks.

PEPERONATA

A healthy Italian appetizer has wonderful eye-appeal. Serve it with bread rounds.

2-3 green bell peppers
2 yellow bell peppers
2 red bell peppers
3 fresh tomatoes, diced
1 tsp. salt
1 tbs. minced fresh parsley
½ cup black olives
2 tbs. capers or chopped anchovies, optional
2 cloves garlic

Cut peppers in half, remove seeds and place peppers under the broiler. Allow skin to turn black; remove from oven and peel off charred skin. Cut peppers into a dice and add to a bowl with tomatoes, salt, parsley, olives and capers. Mash garlic and add to pepper mixture. Chill until ready to serve.

ANTIPASTO GIARDINERIA

This is my favorite antipasto vegetable recipe. I try to make a large batch when the vegetables are at their peak and keep the jars in the refrigerator year-round. Serve this on a platter with a few fresh vegetables like green onion stalks and maybe slices of a good salami.

8 carrots, peeled
8 stalks celery
2 small zucchini
2 red bell peppers
2 green bell peppers
1 small cauliflower
18 small pearl onions (or 2 medium onions, quartered)
5-6 cloves garlic

5-6 small hot dried red chile peppers
½ can (6 oz.) pitted black olives
½ cup pimiento-stuffed green olives
6 cups water
1½ cups white vinegar
2 tbs. salt
2 tbs. mustard seed
1 tsp. celery seed
⅔ cup sugar

Cut carrots, celery and zucchini into uniform 3-inch sticks. Cut peppers in half, remove seeds and cut into ½-inch strips. Break cauliflower into small florets. Fill pint canning jars with a mixture of assorted vegetables. Place 1 clove garlic and 1 hot dried pepper in each jar with both kinds of olives. Pack jar tightly and in an attractive arrangement. Place remaining ingredients in a large pot and boil for 3 minutes. Pour brine mixture into each jar to cover vegetables, clean jar tops well and seal with lids that have been boiled for 3 minutes. Allow jars to "mellow" in the refrigerator for at least 2 weeks before serving.

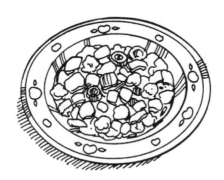

SPINACH-STUFFED MUSHROOMS

Servings: 8-12

The trick in dealing with spinach is to squeeze it very dry; otherwise the filling leaches too much liquid and makes the appetizer too messy to handle.

2 tbs. butter
1/4 cup minced onion
1 cup chopped frozen spinach, defrosted and squeezed dry
1/2 cup low fat ricotta cheese
1/4 cup grated Parmesan cheese
salt and pepper to taste
nutmeg to taste
1 lb. mushrooms

Heat butter in a skillet and sauté onion until limp. Add well-squeezed spinach, ricotta cheese, Parmesan cheese, salt, pepper and nutmeg. Taste and adjust flavor to personal taste. Cut stems from mushrooms just at the cap instead of breaking whole stem off (this helps mushrooms retain shape). Mound filling in centers and bake in a 350° oven for about 20 minutes. Serve warm.

MARINATED BROCCOLI

If desired, this same brine can be used with cauliflower or asparagus.

3 lb. fresh broccoli
¾ cup vinegar (cider or balsamic)
1 tbs. dried dill weed
1 tbs. sugar
1 tbs. salt
1 tsp. pepper
2 cloves garlic, minced
1½ cups chicken broth or vegetable broth

Peel broccoli stems, cut into slender stalks and place in a shallow pan. Mix remaining ingredients together and pour over broccoli. Cover and refrigerate for 24 hours, turning occasionally. Drain vegetables to serve.

STUFFED GRAPE LEAVES

Makes: 48

A Greek favorite is otherwise known as dolmadakia.

1 jar (1 lb.) grape leaves
1 cup minced onion
1/4 cup chicken broth
2 tsp. salt
1 cup uncooked rice
1/2 cup pine nuts
1/2 cup raisins
1 tsp. chopped fresh parsley
1/2 tsp. dill seed
3 cloves garlic, minced

1 tsp. dried oregano
1 tsp. ground cumin
1/2 tsp. allspice
1 tsp. crushed fresh mint
1 cup hot chicken stock
1/3 cup lemon juice
4 cups warm chicken stock
2 tbs. olive oil
sliced lemon wedges for garnish

Wash grape leaves 3 times in cold water to remove brine. Cover leaves with boiling water and soak for 1 hour to make pliable for handling. In a skillet, cook onions for 1 minute to remove excess moisture. Add chicken broth and simmer for 5 minutes. Add 1 tsp. of the salt, rice, pine nuts, raisins, parsley, dill, garlic, oregano, cumin, allspice, mint and chicken stock. Cover and simmer for 10 minutes. Stir in 1/2 of the lemon juice and cool.

Remove thick stem from each grape leaf. Use from 1 tsp. to 1 tbs. filling depending on size of leaves. Place filling at base of leaf on dull side, fold sides of leaf in over filling and roll tightly. (The shiny side of the leaf should be on the outside. If stem end is on the outside, roll the leaf tighter.)

Place a layer of grape leaves on the bottom of a heavy kettle and place rolled dolmadakia in layers in kettle. Pour chicken stock, remaining lemon juice, oil and remaining salt over rolls. Place a heavy plate over rolls to keep them from unrolling and cover with lid. Cook over low heat for 25 minutes (water should be totally absorbed by this time). Place on a platter to cool; garnish. This recipe can actually be frozen if desired.

EGGPLANT CAVIAR

Makes: 1 quart

Hollow out an eggplant or colorful long squashes and fill with this healthy mixture. Serve with an assortment of crackers or bread.

2 eggplants
1 tbs. olive oil
2 cloves garlic
1 small onion
1 red bell pepper, seeded
1 green bell pepper, seeded
1 tomato, peeled and seeded
1 tbs. capers
1 tbs. fresh lemon juice
1/8 tsp. Tabasco Sauce
1 tsp. salt
1/4 tsp. pepper
3 tbs. vinegar (prefer balsamic)
1 tsp. basil
1/4 cup olive oil or vegetable broth
1/2 cup chopped black olives
1/2 cup chopped green olives

Brush eggplants with olive oil and bake in a 350° oven for 30 minutes (or until they begin to soften). Remove from oven, cut in half and scoop out flesh. Save eggplant shell if you wish to serve the dip in it. In a food processor or blender, chop garlic; add onion and bell peppers. Pulse on and off to coarsely chop vegetables. Remove chopped vegetables and set aside. Add tomato, eggplant pulp, capers, lemon juice, Tabasco, salt, pepper, vinegar, basil and oil to processor or blender and process until well mixed. Add coarsely chopped vegetables and process just until mixed. Transfer vegetables to a heavy saucepan and cook over medium heat for 20 minutes. Add chopped olives, taste and adjust seasonings, and chill. Serve in a hollowed-out eggplant shell or squash or colorful dish.

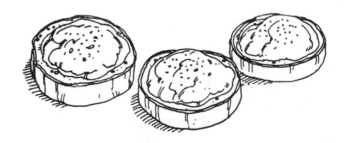

BABA GHANOUSH

An eggplant puree specialty that is very healthy and tasty originated in the Middle East. The trick to this dish is in the smoky flavor obtained from scraping the charred skins. If you prefer a little heat, add a dash of cayenne for variety. This is good as a dip or spread for pita or Middle Eastern flatbread.

2 large eggplants
salt to taste
2 cloves garlic, finely minced
1/4 cup chopped onion
lime or lemon juice to taste
1 1/2 tbs. tahini (sesame seed paste)
2 tbs. chopped fresh parsley

Wash and dry eggplants, and split in half. Place cut-side down on a baking sheet. Broil eggplants for 15 to 20 minutes, allowing skin to blacken considerably and flesh to soften. Remove from oven, sprinkle cut side with salt and put eggplant in a colander to drain for about 15 minutes to remove excess moisture. Scrap pulp from eggplant rind, being sure to scrap some of the charred bits into mixture for flavor. Place pulp and remaining ingredients in a food processor or blender and puree until smooth. Taste and adjust seasonings. Refrigerate until ready to serve.

SWEET POTATO AND CARROT DIP

Makes: 4 cups

Dip into this piquant, yet sweet, vegetable dip with vegetables or pita bread. For a healthy alternative, rather than boiling the vegetables, steam them until tender and add a sprinkling of salt for flavor.

1 lb. sweet potatoes or yams
1 lb. carrots
water to cover
1 tsp. salt
3 cloves garlic
1 tsp. ground cumin
1 tsp. cinnamon
3-4 tbs. olive oil or vegetable broth
3 tbs. vinegar (prefer balsamic)
1 pinch cayenne pepper, or more to taste

Peel sweet potatoes and carrots and cut into pieces. Place in a saucepan, cover with water, add salt and boil until vegetables are soft. Drain. Puree cooked vegetables in a food processor or blender until smooth. Add remaining ingredients and puree until blended. Taste and adjust seasonings to your personal preference.

SALSA

It's a must to serve salsa with tortilla chips (freshly made if you've got the time). It's also good with bean dishes, vegetable salads and chicken. For a low fat dipper, cut corn tortillas into wedges and bake in a 350° oven for 10 minutes or until crisp.

1 medium sweet onion, chopped (preferably Bermuda variety)
3 cloves garlic, minced
½ green bell pepper, chopped
½ red bell pepper, chopped
½ cup chopped fresh cilantro
2 tbs. lemon juice
2 tsp. sugar
2 cups fresh seeded tomatoes, or 1 can (15 oz.) Mexican-style stewed tomatoes
salt and pepper to taste
chopped fresh jalapeño chiles to taste, optional

Place all ingredients in a food processor or blender. Process with pulsing action until just blended. Do not puree mixture; texture should be chunky. Taste and adjust seasonings.

DILLED BROCCOLI AND CARROTS

This simple, colorful appetizer could be used as a vegetable side dish. To make it even leaner, use 2 tbs. chicken broth instead of the butter and vegetable oil.

1 tbs. butter
1 tbs. vegetable oil
3-4 medium carrots, peeled and sliced
2 tbs. dry white wine
½ medium onion, sliced
1 cup fresh broccoli florets
½ tsp. dried dill weed
pepper to taste

In a large skillet, heat butter and oil and sauté carrots for 1 minute. Add wine, cover and cook over medium heat for 5 minutes. Add remaining ingredients, cover and simmer for 5 minutes or until vegetables are tender-crisp. Serve warm with toothpicks.

LOW FAT CUCUMBER DIP

This refreshing dip goes well with vegetables or crackers.

1 medium cucumber, peeled
salt
1/3 cup low fat or nonfat cottage cheese
1 cup plain low fat or nonfat yogurt
1 tbs. chopped fresh parsley
1/2 tsp. dried dill weed
1/4 tsp. white pepper

Cut cucumber in half, discard seeds and shred. Sprinkle cucumber with salt and drain in a colander for 30 minutes. Place cucumber shreds in a paper towel and squeeze dry. Place remaining ingredients in a food processor or blender and process until smooth. Stir in cucumber, taste and adjust seasonings. Cover and refrigerate until ready to serve.

CHUTNEY-STUFFED CELERY

A delightful change for stuffed celery has a spicy, sweet flavor.

1 bunch celery
8 oz. low fat or nonfat cream cheese, softened
1 tsp. white vinegar
1 tsp. curry powder
6 tbs. mango chutney, finely chopped
1-2 tbs. milk

Separate celery ribs, strip off any tough strands and chill until about 1 hour before serving. With a mixer, blend remaining ingredients together, using milk to thin to a thick but spreadable consistency. Taste and adjust seasonings. Stuff mixture into celery stalks, chill for a short while, cut into 2-inch pieces and serve.

BAKED VEGETABLE
AND CHICKEN WON TONS

Won ton wrappers are fat-free and serve as a good alternative to flaky pastry recipes. Turkey can be substituted for the chicken if desired.

8 oz. ground raw chicken
1/4 cup chopped celery
1/2 cup shredded carrots
1 tbs. sherry
2 tsp. grated ginger root
1 tbs. soy sauce

2 tsp. cornstarch
1/3 cup bottled plum or sweet and sour sauce
24 square won ton wrappers
nonstick cooking spray

In a skillet, sauté chicken with celery and carrots for several minutes. Stir in sherry, ginger root, soy sauce, cornstarch and plum sauce. Remove from heat and allow to cool to room temperature. Moisten edges of won ton wrapper, place a rounded teaspoon of filling in the center and pinch opposite ends together to seal. Spray baking sheet with nonstick cooking spray. Place filled won tons on sheet and spray lightly with nonstick cooking spray. Bake in a 375° oven for 10 minutes or until brown and crisp.

SALMON MOUSSE

I like to use a mold in the shape of a fish or shell with this recipe. Surround the molded mousse with greens and lemon slices.

2 pkg. (¼ oz. each) unflavored
  gelatin
½ cup cold water
1 cup boiling water
¾ cup low fat or nonfat mayonnaise
2 cans (1 lb. each) salmon, drained
1 tsp. lemon juice

1 tbs. grated onion
1 tbs. Worcestershire sauce
1 tsp. salt
¼ tsp. pepper
8 oz. low fat or nonfat sour cream
fresh parsley sprigs and lemon slices
  for garnish

Soak gelatin in cold water until dissolved. Add boiling water, stir and let cool until thickened. Beat mayonnaise into gelatin mixture until frothy. Break up salmon and remove skin and bones. Add to gelatin mixture with lemon juice, onion, Worcestershire sauce, salt and pepper. Fold in sour cream. Pour into a lightly oiled 6- to 8-cup mold and chill until firm. Unmold onto a platter and garnish with parsley sprigs and lemon slices.

BAKED CLAMS

To create a dramatic presentation, arrange the clams on the half-shell on an ovenproof serving platter that is covered with rock salt.

40 clams
1/4 cup water
1/2 cup finely chopped fresh parsley
4 cloves garlic, minced
1/2 cup breadcrumbs
1/4 cup olive oil or chicken broth
1/2 tsp. dried oregano
salt and pepper to taste

Place clams in a pan with water, cover and steam for 2 minutes. Snap off each top shell and discard. Arrange clams on the half-shell on an ovenproof serving platter (on bed of rock salt if desired). Mix remaining ingredients together, taste and adjust seasonings. Place a small amount of mixture over each clam and place under the broiler until heated through and browned. Serve immediately.

FRUIT KABOBS

Fruit makes a refreshing appetizer that is ideal served in the summer months. Kids especially love this one. Be inventive about the possible dipping sauces.

3 bananas
3 apples
2 tbs. lemon juice in 1 cup cold water
3 kiwis

2 oranges
1 melon (cantaloupe, honeydew, watermelon, etc.)
1 cup fresh or canned pineapple chunks

DIPPING SAUCE ALTERNATIVES
nonfat sour cream mixed with orange juice and honey
low fat or nonfat flavored yogurt
plain yogurt flavored with extracts

granola for rolling kabobs, optional

Peel and cut bananas into chunks. Core apples, peel if desired, and cut into large chunks. Dip bananas and apples in lemon juice mixture to prevent darkening. Remove peelings from kiwis and cut into chunks. Peel oranges and divide into segments. Cut melon into cubes. Place prepared fruits on wooden skewers, alternating variety. Refrigerate until ready to serve. Serve with dipping sauce and granola if desired.

CREAMY STUFFED DATES

This recipe is quick and easy. Garnish with twisted slices of orange and a few mint sprigs.

40 whole pitted dates
8 oz. low fat or nonfat cream cheese, softened
1/3 cup orange liqueur
sugar to taste, optional
2 tbs. grated fresh orange peel (zest)

Cut dates in half lengthwise and place on a serving platter. Mix cream cheese with orange liqueur, taste and adjust flavor. If desired, a little sugar can be added to taste. Place cream cheese mixture into a piping bag and pipe into date halves. Sprinkle with grated orange peel.

DIPS AND SPREADS

Dips and spreads should be nutritious, interesting and flavorful. The advantage of dips and spreads is that they can be made ahead of time and can serve large numbers. Serve them in attractive dishes surrounded by one or several of the following: bread slices, pita, toast, crackers, chips, pretzels, fresh fruits, cooked meat cubes, marinated or fresh vegetables.

ROASTED RED PEPPER DIP

Makes: 2½ cups

Roasted red peppers are very similar to pimientos. Serve this dip with a beautiful array of fresh vegetables and garnish with fresh flowers and herbs.

2 green onions, chopped
1 jar (15 oz.) roasted red peppers, drained
1-2 tbs. lemon juice
1 cup whipped cream cheese

In a food processor or blender, chop green onions finely. Add remaining ingredients and process to make a coarse puree. Chill until ready to use.

CREAMY AVOCADO VEGGIE DIP

Makes: 2½ cups

Create a gorgeous array of colorful vegetables to serve beside this delicious dip. It also goes well with tortilla chips or crisp bagel chips.

1½ tbs. red wine vinegar (prefer balsamic)
1½ tbs. lemon juice
½ cup olive oil
1 tbs. Dijon mustard
¼ cup minced green onions
1 tsp. salt

½ tsp. sugar
freshly ground pepper to taste
8 oz. cream cheese, softened
2 cloves garlic, minced
1 large ripe avocado, pit removed
2 tbs. chopped fresh parsley

In a food processor or blender, place vinegar, lemon juice, olive oil, mustard, 2 tbs. of the green onions, salt, sugar and pepper. Process until smooth. Remove mixture and set aside. Place cream cheese, garlic and avocado in food processor and process until smooth and creamy. Very slowly drip vinegar mixture into cream cheese mixture while machine is running. Blend or process until smooth. Transfer to a serving bowl and stir in remaining 2 tbs. green onions and parsley for color and texture.

BAGNA CAUDA

Say BON yuh COW duh. This is a creamy variation of a traditional Italian garlic dip that goes well with vegetables or bread rounds for dipping.

1/4 cup butter
6-8 anchovy fillets, finely chopped
4 cloves garlic, minced
2 cups heavy cream
1 tbs. cornstarch
2 tbs. water

Melt butter in a saucepan and add chopped anchovies and garlic. Sauté for a few minutes. Add cream and heat to almost a boil. Mix cornstarch with water and add to cream mixture, stirring until thickened. Remove from heat and serve immediately.

GUACAMOLE

Save the avocado pit and imbed it in the center of the mixture until ready to serve — this will help to keep the dip from becoming dark. Serve with tortilla chips, corn chips, vegetables or plain tortillas.

4 large ripe avocados, peeled and pitted
juice of 2 limes
½ cup shredded cheddar cheese
½ cup chopped Bermuda onion
dash salt
1 jalapeño pepper, chopped, optional
1 tbs. chopped fresh cilantro
1-2 tomatoes, seeded and chopped
chopped fresh cilantro for garnish

In a food processor or blender, blend 3 of the avocados until smooth. Add juice, cheese, onion, salt, jalapeño and 1 tbs. cilantro. Taste and adjust seasonings. Chop remaining avocado. Stir in chopped tomatoes and remaining chopped avocado, which will add a chunky texture to mixture. Sprinkle with cilantro.

HUMMUS DIP

This is quick to put together and is ideally served with fresh or toasted pita bread. Tahini is sesame seed paste and can now be found in most grocery and health food stores.

1 tbs. olive oil
1 small onion, chopped
2-3 cloves garlic, minced
2 cups canned garbanzo beans
½ tsp. turmeric
2 tbs. chopped fresh parsley
1-2 tbs. lemon juice, to taste
2-3 tbs. tahini, optional

Heat olive oil in a skillet and sauté onion and garlic until soft and transparent. Rinse garbanzo beans with cold water and drain. Place all ingredients in a blender or food processor and puree until the consistency resembles that of mayonnaise.

CLAM DIP

Because of the uncomplicated recipe, the clam flavor can be fully appreciated. This one is quick and simple. Serve with chips, crackers or bread rounds.

1 can (6 oz.) minced clams
8 oz. cream cheese, softened
1 tbs. Worcestershire sauce
1 tsp. lemon juice

Drain clams and reserve juice. Mix together clams, cream cheese, Worcestershire sauce and lemon juice. Taste and add more lemon juice if desired. If you wish a thinner dip, add a small amount of clam juice until desired consistency is reached.

CRAB FONDUE

Makes: 3 cups

This delicious creamy dip is best served with French bread rounds or plain crackers. Serve warm in a chafing dish.

2 tbs. butter
½ cup chopped mushrooms
¼ cup cream sherry
salt and pepper to taste
dash cayenne pepper
enough paprika to color
3 egg yolks
1 cup cream
1 lb. crabmeat

Melt butter in a skillet and sauté mushrooms until tender. Add sherry, salt, pepper, cayenne, and paprika and stir to combine. Stir in egg yolks and cream and stir over medium heat until mixture thickens. Stir in crabmeat and serve warm.

OLIVE SPREAD

Otherwise known as "tapenade." This is a perfect dish to take to a party. Cut little baguettes into small rounds or serve with freshly made breadsticks.

2 cans (6 oz. each) pitted black olives
3 tbs. capers
½ cup minced onion
1 tsp. minced garlic
2 tbs. chopped fresh parsley
¼ cup grated Parmesan cheese
2 tbs. olive oil
2 tbs. vinegar (prefer balsamic)
½ tsp. salt
½ tsp. pepper
¼ cup chopped red bell pepper

In a food processor or blender, just barely chop olives; remove and set aside. Place remaining ingredients in processor, except 2 tbs. of the red bell pepper. Chop into a fine blend; stir mixture into olives. Taste and adjust seasonings. Sprinkle remaining chopped red pepper on top for garnish.

AVOCADO OLIVE SPREAD

Makes: 3 cups

This spread can be served hot, spread on toasted bread rounds with Swiss cheese melted on top, or cold, served with raw vegetables.

12 oz. cream cheese, softened
1 ripe avocado (prefer Haas variety)
1 tsp. lemon juice
1 cup finely chopped black olives
1 tbs. chopped fresh parsley
1/3 cup chopped tomatoes
1/4 cup finely chopped celery

Place cream cheese in a food processor or use a mixer and blend until smooth. Peel avocado, remove pit and mash with lemon juice. Add to cream cheese and puree until smooth. Add remaining ingredients and barely mix to combine. Chill until ready to use.

THREE PEPPER SPREAD

A quick, colorful, hot dip goes well with crackers, pita crisps or bagel chips.

8 oz. cream cheese, softened
½ cup shredded Parmesan cheese
1 small onion, diced
1 tbs. chopped fresh basil
1 red bell pepper
1 green bell pepper
1 yellow bell pepper

Using a food processor or blender, process cream cheese and Parmesan until fluffy. Add onion and basil and mix to combine. Seed and cut peppers into chunks. Add to cream cheese mixture and process until well combined. Place in a shallow baking dish and bake in a 350° oven for 15 minutes.

CHUTNEY AND CHEESE SPREAD

Makes: 3 cups

Chutney creates a spicy, savory taste sensation. Curry is an acquired taste, so be conservative unless you know your guests appreciate it. Serve with crisp crackers.

8 oz. cream cheese, softened
4 oz. cheddar cheese, shredded
2 tbs. brandy
1 tsp. curry powder, or to taste
8 oz. jar mango chutney
½ cup toasted chopped toasted almonds
2 chopped green onions

In a food processor or with a mixer, beat cream cheese, cheddar cheese, brandy and curry until light and fluffy. Taste and adjust seasonings. Pack into a pretty serving dish and cover with chutney. Chill until ready to serve. Sprinkle with chopped almonds and green onions.

GELATIN CHEESE SPREAD

Makes: 3 cups

Serve this in the center of a large platter surrounded by fresh vegetables and/or crackers.

6 oz. cheese crackers or Ritz crackers, crushed
1 envelope (1/4 oz.) unflavored gelatin
1/4 cup cold water
2 cups sour cream
1 pkg. (6 oz.) Italian dry salad dressing mix
1/4 cup crumbled blue cheese
2 cups small curd cottage cheese

Butter a 9-inch springform pan. Press cracker crumbs in bottom and set aside. Mix gelatin with cold water and warm gently in a small saucepan until dissolved. Blend remaining ingredients in a food processor or blender until smooth and add dissolved gelatin. Pour into prepared springform pan, cover and chill for several hours to set. To serve, invert on a platter and remove pan sides and bottom.

CRUNCHY HAM AND CHEESE BALL

Ham dominates the flavor of this cheese ball instead of cheddar cheese. Always wait until the last hour before rolling cheese balls in nuts, so the nuts will maintain their crunchy quality and full flavor. Serve with an assortment of crackers.

8 oz. cream cheese, softened
¼ cup mayonnaise
1 green onion, finely diced
2 tbs. chopped fresh parsley
¼ tsp. dry mustard
¼ tsp. Tabasco Sauce
2 cups grated cooked ham
1 cup chopped toasted walnuts

Using a food processor or mixer, mix all ingredients together, except nuts. Form into a ball and chill until ready to serve. Just before serving, roll in nuts.

CRAB PATÉ

This fresh-tasting, elegant appetizer should be served with plain crackers or bread rounds so the delicate flavor of the crab can be fully appreciated.

3 hard-cooked egg yolks
½ cup butter
½ cup mayonnaise
1 clove garlic, minced
1 tsp. Dijon mustard
dash horseradish sauce

¼ cup minced green onion
¼ cup minced fresh parsley
12 oz. fresh crabmeat
2 tbs. lemon juice
salt and white pepper to taste

In a food processor or blender, combine egg yolks, butter, mayonnaise, garlic, mustard, horseradish, green onion and parsley and process until smooth. Place mixture in a bowl and add crabmeat, lemon juice, salt and white pepper. Stir gently to combine. Taste and adjust seasonings. Place in a covered container and refrigerate until ready to serve.

CRAB AND AVOCADO MOLDED SPREAD

Makes: 3½ cups

This is a delicious chilled dish that can be molded for a beautiful presentation. If feeling extravagant, use extra crabmeat to garnish center and edges. Serve with crackers or crispy toast rounds.

1 cup water
2 pkg. (¼ oz. each) unflavored
  gelatin
4 ripe avocados
1 cup mayonnaise
1 cup sour cream
2-3 tbs. finely minced onion

¼ cup lemon juice
1 tsp. salt
dash cayenne pepper
½ tsp. Dijon mustard
18 oz. crabmeat
additional crabmeat for garnish, optional

Mix water and gelatin together, stirring to dissolve. Gently bring to a boil and set aside to cool. Mash avocados and stir into cooled gelatin with remaining ingredients, except crabmeat. Gently fold in crabmeat and pour mixture into an oiled 4-cup mold. Cover and refrigerate for 8 hours. Unmold and garnish as desired.

CRABMEAT SPREAD

A quick and elegant dish goes well with special crackers, crusty bread rounds or melba toast. If desired, save a few whole crab legs for garnish.

8 oz. cream cheese, softened
2 green onions, finely chopped
2 tbs. lemon juice
1/4 tsp. paprika
1/4 tsp. white pepper
1/8 tsp. cayenne pepper
1/4 tsp. salt
12 oz. crabmeat

Place all ingredients, except crabmeat, in a food processor or blender and process until smooth. Transfer mixture to a serving bowl and stir in crabmeat. Chill until ready to serve.

SIMPLE LIVER PATÉ

A traditional way to serve paté is accompanied with cocktail onions, gherkins and of course, crusty French bread.

1 lb. bacon
1½ cups chopped onions
1 lb. calf's liver, cut into 1-inch cubes
1 lb. chicken livers, cut in half
2 tsp. salt, or to taste
1 tsp. pepper
3 egg yolks
2 eggs
¼ cup red wine (prefer Madeira)
¾ tsp. chervil
½ tsp. tarragon
½ tsp. nutmeg
¼ tsp. allspice

Preheat oven to 375°. Line a loaf pan or a 7-inch soufflé mold with bacon slices, reserving 6 slices for cooking. Dice 6 reserved bacon slices and fry in a skillet until brown. Add onions and sauté until onions are slightly browned. Add calf's liver and chicken livers with 1 tsp. of the salt and ½ tsp. of the pepper and sauté until no longer pink.

Using a food processor or blender, puree entire mixture, a little at a time, until smooth. Add egg yolks, eggs, red wine, spices, and remaining salt and pepper. Process until combined. Taste and adjust seasonings. Pour mixture into bacon-lined baking dish and cover with foil. Place pan in a water bath: set it in a larger baking pan and add water halfway up sides of filled pan. Bake for 2 hours. Remove from oven, pour off any excess oil and allow to cool. Place a weight, like a brick or heavy pottery, on top of paté and refrigerate for at least 8 hours before serving.

APRICOT SPREAD

Serve this sweet spread with tea breads or mixed with cream cheese to serve as a spread for mini-bagels.

1 lb. dried apricots
enough apple or apricot juice to cover
1 pinch anise
2 tbs. arrowroot or cornstarch
2 cups apple juice
1 pinch salt

Place apricots in a heavy saucepan, cover with juice and add anise. Simmer on low until soft, about 30 minutes. Transfer to a food processor or blender and puree. Mix arrowroot or cornstarch with 2 cups apple juice, place in saucepan with pureed apricots and stir until thickened. Add salt. Taste and adjust seasonings. Refrigerate until ready to use.

INDEX

SERVE CREATIVE, EASY, NUTRITIOUS MEALS WITH Nitty Gritty® COOKBOOKS

Sautés
Cooking in Porcelain
Appetizers
Recipes for the Loaf Pan
Casseroles
The Best Bagels are made at home*
   (*perfect for your bread machine)
The Toaster Oven Cookbook
Skewer Cooking on the Grill
Creative Mexican Cooking
Extra-Special Crockery Pot Recipes
Cooking in Clay
Marinades
Deep Fried Indulgences
Cooking with Parchment Paper
The Garlic Cookbook
Flatbreads From Around the World
From Your Ice Cream Maker
Favorite Cookie Recipes
Cappuccino/Espresso: The Book of
   Beverages
Indoor Grilling

Slow Cooking
The Best Pizza is made at home*
   (*perfect for your bread machine)
The Well Dressed Potato
Convection Oven Cookery
The Steamer Cookbook
The Pasta Machine Cookbook
The Versatile Rice Cooker
The Dehydrator Cookbook
The Bread Machine Cookbook
The Bread Machine Cookbook II
The Bread Machine Cookbook III
The Bread Machine Cookbook IV:
   Whole Grains and Natural Sugars
The Bread Machine Cookbook V:
   Favorite Recipes from 100 Kitchens
The Bread Machine Cookbook VI:
   *Hand-Shaped Breads from the
   Dough Cycle*
Worldwide Sourdoughs From Your
   Bread Machine
Recipes for the Pressure Cooker

The New Blender Book
The Sandwich Maker Cookbook
Waffles
The Coffee Book
The Juicer Book
The Juicer Book II
Bread Baking (traditional)
No Salt, No Sugar, No Fat Cookbook
Cooking for 1 or 2
Quick and Easy Pasta Recipes
The 9x13 Pan Cookbook
Extra-Special Crockery Pot Recipes
Low Fat American Favorites
Now That's Italian!
Fabulous Fiber Cookery
Low Salt, Low Sugar, Low Fat Desserts
Healthy Cooking on the Run
Muffins, Nut Breads and More
The Wok
New Ways to Enjoy Chicken
Favorite Seafood Recipes
New International Fondue Cookbook

For a free catalog, write or call:
Bristol Publishing Enterprises, Inc.
P.O. Box 1737
San Leandro, CA 94577
(800) 346-4889; in California, (510) 895-4461